TWO MEN FROM MALTA

TWO MEN FROM MALTA

A Shipwrecked Apostle
and
A Canadian Newspaperman

*Passionately Appeal to Roman Catholics
To Examine their Faith*

JOE SERGE

with Dr. Joel Nederhood

Solid Ground Christian Books
Birmingham, Alabama USA

Solid Ground Christian Books
PO Box 660132
Vestavia Hills AL 35266
sgcb@charter.net
www.solid-ground-books.com
205-443-0311

TWO MEN FROM MALTA

A Shipwrecked Apostle and a Canadian Newspaperman
Passionately Appeal to Roman Catholics to Examine their Faith

Joe Serge with Dr. Joel Nederhood

Cover image is the famous painting *The Shipwreck* by William Turner (1805)

Cover design by Borgo Design of Tuscaloosa, Alabama.
Contact them at borgogirl@bellsouth.net

ISBN: 1-59925-124-8

To Nicole,
my wife and companion
on the Road to Damascus

TABLE OF CONTENTS

Foreword

Two Men from Malta—one of the men is the Apostle Paul, the other is Joe Serge, a Toronto newspaperman and columnist. In this book Serge describes his odyssey from Roman Catholicism to the faith of the Reformation.

Serge invited Joel Nederhood, a theologian and long time radio and television teacher, to join him in examining primary Roman teaching such as "the Mass," "Mary," "the Papacy," and the essence of salvation itself. Dr. Nederhood, whose published works include *This Splendid Journey* and *The Forever People*, has produced a highly readable and provocative examination of the biblical material that Roman Catholic believers should consider as they evaluate their faith position.

This book conveys the high sense of freedom that Joe Serge experiences now that he has embraced the biblical teachings of salvation by grace alone, apart from works. The book also conveys sincere respect for Roman Catholics who will read it. And there can be no question that Joe Serge is praying that many who read *Two Men from Malta* will join him in following the biblical teaching that reveals that Christ's works, not ours, will bring sinners into glory.

I

TWO MEN FROM MALTA

When the water soaked apostle stumbled from the fierce and cruel waters of the Mediterranean onto Malta's rocky shore, there's a good chance some of my ancestors gave him a hand and wrapped him in a blanket. Later, they would have joined those around the campfire who gasped when the bonfire viper fastened its fangs in Paul's arm: "Ah yes," they said to one another, "this man is a vicious criminal and though he escaped the storm and the shipwreck with his life, the great god Justice will now punish him with death." But when the apostle Paul stripped the viper off his arm and failed to die, they began to revere him. And when they heard him tell them about Jesus of Nazareth, they marveled even more.

I don't know whether any of my ancestors believed in Jesus when they heard Paul, but I do know that nineteen centuries later when I learned Paul's message about Jesus my life changed completely.

Paul's Malta experience has always intrigued me because my family tree is rooted in the thin soil of that island nation. In the Bible, Acts 27 tells about Paul's harrowing voyage on a wheat ship that weathered a two-week hurricane before it broke up on rocks off the Malta coast. Sailors who read Acts 27 are astonished by the accurate detail of that nautical adventure; when I read it, I am fascinated by the thought that some of my forebears saw the great apostle when the shipwrecked survivors washed ashore on Malta. Possibly some of them did believe in Christ when Paul spoke of him. I hope so. One thing I know: once I saw the way of salvation that God had revealed to Paul, I had to examine everything I had ever thought was true about the way a sinner like me could go to heaven.

My meeting with Paul was very ordinary. One morning, shortly after five, I stumbled out of bed at my home near Toronto and made my first cup of coffee. As I channel-surfed, *Faith 20,* a half hour program sponsored by the Christian Reformed Church, caught my attention. In spite of myself, I found myself paying attention to Joel Nederhood's message, and during the next several weeks I taped it and listened to it later in the day.

Faith 20 was a quiet program; it was by no means an attack on other forms of Christianity—it simply brought the biblical message of salvation over and over again. As I listened, I began to see that I needed to examine what I had been taught about salvation. In fact, the message of the Apostle Paul, contained in Bible books like Romans and Galatians, is a gospel that is different from the "gospel" I was taught as a kid. I began to see that the gospel I was taught was actually not a gospel but a doctrinal system that made me uncertain about my salvation rather than sure of it. It made me dependent on the church. I realized that I had to make changes.

As a Roman Catholic, my primary concern was that I would be sufficiently pleasing to God the hour of my death to insure that I would not go to hell nor have to spend a long time in purgatory before I would enter eternal life. I figured that escaping hell and cutting down on purgatory time depended on how I looked to God the day of my death. If He saw that I had done enough good works to merit heaven and had no lingering guilt of mortal (serious) sin, the gates would swing open. Heaven depended on my life quality. The equation was simple: *be good* = *be saved*. Makes sense. But this equation is dead wrong.

As the biblical way of salvation became clear to me, I learned that salvation—eternal life—does not depend on how good we are but depends on how good Jesus Christ is. I was surprised to learn that the Bible tells us that when we believe in Jesus Christ as Savior and Lord, his righteousness becomes our righteousness. I discovered that when I asked God to forgive me, solely because of what Jesus achieved on Calvary's cross, all my sins were blotted out. I learned that the Bible tells me that if I believe in Christ, God looks at me as a person who is wearing the righteousness of Christ. His obedience becomes my obedience.

This means that when I die, the heaven and hell question will not be: *How good am I?* Rather it will be: *What is my relationship to Jesus Christ? Do I believe in him?*

What does believing in Jesus mean? It means believing that Jesus Christ is the Son of God. It means confessing my sins to God, repenting of my sins and believing that Jesus paid everything I owe God—believing he paid my debt of sin.

I found out that even though I remain a sinner all of my life, the Holy Spirit will help me fight against sin. The central point, as I saw it once I began to know the Bible, is that salvation is from God, first, last and everything in between.

I was shaken by the biblical message *Faith 20* kept telling me. From childhood I had assumed that whatever the Roman Church taught me was true—the Pope was God's representative on earth, and what the priest told me should not be questioned. I even believed that priests had the power to forgive sins. I also believed that attendance at mass and regular prayers to Mary and other saints would keep me pointed in the right direction.

All my life I believed in the supernatural powers of medals and relics and in the great benefits obtained through pilgrimages to holy shrines that honored Mary and other saints. I believed in grace, but, to be honest, when I thought about grace, it had nothing to do with salvation. I considered grace as a blessing I received when I pleased God—the more

13

I pleased him, the more he would bless me. For example, I would say things like, "by God's grace, he had a wonderful family," or "by God's grace he was healthy into old age," or, "by God's grace, he escaped harm in the accident."

As I began to study the Bible, I realized that deep down I was actually very nervous about my salvation. I had been taught that baptism washed away the sin I was born with, often called *original sin*, but that I was responsible to do something to make up for sins I committed after baptism. I had to confess sins to a priest and do good works. I wondered if I could accumulate enough good works during my life that God would not only find me worthy of heaven, but also that I would spend little or no time at all in purgatory.

The thought never entered my head to fall on my knees and thank God that he had fully paid for my sin through the crucifixion of his Son the Lord Jesus 2000 years before I was born. I was totally blind to God's free offer of salvation through faith in Jesus Christ.

Though I had an expensive, hardcover Bible, I never read it. I assumed that the Bible was for the church to read and interpret; it was the church's duty to tell people like me what was in it and what it meant. I thought that as long as I went to mass regularly, I was on the right track. At mass I always heard a little bit from the Bible because the priest read it for me, and that was enough, as far as I was concerned.

But then I met the apostle Paul, and I began to read the books of the Bible he wrote. And I read the gospels that tell us about the life and teaching of Jesus Christ. I found that I could understand what was on those exciting pages. And I found that what was on those pages contradicted much of what I had been taught. I came to the terrifying conclusion that the Bible contradicted many of my Roman Catholic beliefs.

Whoa! Thud! I guess you would have to say that I fell off my horse the same way Paul did one day when he was on

TWO MEN FROM MALTA

one of his search and destroy missions to imprison Christians.
Let me tell you what happened to him.

II

THE CONVERSION OF A CHRIST-HATER

A great proof that the Bible is true and Christianity is a special work of the one true God is the fact that the most important person in the New Testament, after the Lord Jesus Christ Himself, is a person who hated Christ with fierce passion.

People like us cannot imagine the intensity of Paul's reaction to the person and work of Jesus of Nazareth. Everything about Jesus was the very opposite of what Paul believed true religion actually was.

As I tell you about this, let me call Paul by the name he used when he was a Christ-hater: *Saul.* First of all, Saul hated Jesus because of his humble origin. Nazareth was a crummy, two-bit town, contaminated by too many Gentiles, situated far from the center of Jewish religious life. The very idea that the Messiah of Israel would come from such a God-forsaken place made Saul sick to his stomach.

Second, Saul hated Jesus because Jesus deliberately and repeatedly declared that the way of salvation that Saul and his friends followed was going to drag them into hell instead of lift them to heaven. Saul was a member of a proud religious sect, the Pharisees. They studied the law of God, they enlarged on the law of God, they improved on the law of God and they prided themselves on keeping the law of God as perfectly as human beings could. These Pharisees considered themselves Abraham's super-children who would surely go to heaven because every heartbeat sent Abraham's blood through their veins and because they kept the law so well.

More than anything else, the Pharisees were strict about the way they kept the Sabbath—they did no work whatsoever on the Sabbath—none—zero—zilch. But Jesus of Nazareth went out of his way to do many of his miracles on the Sabbath day, and when he did that, it was like telling the Pharisees that they didn't understand the very law they kept so carefully. Saul was furious.

The third reason that Saul hated Jesus with such passion was that (now get this) this man from Nazareth, who obviously had no understanding of God's law, actually called God his Father. He was serious. He displayed his divinity by working astonishing miracles. And what was even worse, he forgave sins. Saul and his fellow Pharisees knew that only God can forgive sins. They charged Jesus with committing blasphemy, the worst sin a person can commit. Could anything be more shocking than to have a man from Galilee say he was God's Son and then act as if it was really true?

It was the happiest day of Saul's life when he heard that Jesus of Nazareth had finally been executed in the cruelest way—by crucifixion. Finally God's earth was rid of this unspeakable scum. But then, wonder of wonders, his followers claimed that this filthy corruption of the human race had risen from the grave and had appeared to his followers for forty days after the resurrection. Then, of all things, they said he ascended into heaven, and then (ohhhhh, what horror!) he sent his Holy Spirit back into the church who then transformed his followers into powerful witnesses and miracle workers.

Hear, O Israel, the Lord your God, the Lord is one. This statement had been burned into Saul's mind, and now there were people out there who said that this one God existed in three persons, The Father, The Son, and the Holy Spirit. And one of those persons, they were saying, was Jesus of Nazareth. Even to think such a thing was outrageous.

Jesus of Nazareth—just repeating his name was more than Saul could handle. His hatred of Jesus consumed him. He would not rest day or night in his pursuit of Jesus' followers—apostles, prophets, teachers and ordinary believers. When one of them was being stoned to death, he cheered the executioners on and held their coats while they committed murder.

Do you get the picture? Saul hated Jesus because of who he said he was, because of the way he broke God's law, and because he opposed the way of salvation to which Saul was totally committed. Saul believed that we are saved through our works. If we were to put this in theological terms, we could say that Saul had a Roman Catholic soteriology. Soteriology is the theology of salvation. The Roman Catholic Church teaches that we are saved through God's grace *plus* our works. That's exactly what Saul believed before he was converted.

It happened on one of his persecution trips. He was headed toward the city of Damascus with warrants for the arrests of Christians in his pocket when, at high noon, the sun exploded, and he was thrown from his mount to the ground. From out of the center of the glorious brilliance, the words of the exalted Savior sounded, clear and terrifying: "Saul, Saul, why are you persecuting me?"

"Who are you, Lord?" he called.

"I am Jesus of Nazareth, whom you are persecuting," came the stunning reply.

It was true! It was all true! Jesus of Nazareth was actually the Son of God, and he was alive, and his irresistible power was in control. In a nano-second Saul's former world collapsed and another world rose up in its place. Jesus is the Christ, the Son of God. Jesus is Lord. The Holy Spirit of the risen Christ entered Saul's heart and, as we say, *the rest is history.* Even his name was changed: now we know *Saul* the persecutor of Christ's followers as *Paul,* the man who gave the rest of his life calling people like me and my ancestors to faith in the risen Lord.

Paul now knew that his former enemy was his Savior and friend; he was thankful that Jesus of Nazareth had not killed him on the spot. Over time, the full message of the truth about Jesus Christ was revealed to him. Along with everything else, he saw that the way of salvation through the works of the law was steaming, stinking garbage that had to be disposed of as quickly as possible. He saw that the very cross that he had despised was the centerpiece of God's salvation. He saw that salvation is not by works but it is by God's grace, and by that grace alone. Alone.

As I thought about how the greatest persecutor of the Christ's people became the greatest missionary of the church, I could not rest until I learned more of the way of salvation God had equipped Paul to preach to the world. I began to see that the way of salvation by grace alone was different from what I had been taught. Admittedly, my conversion was by no means as dramatic as Paul's, but for me it was an "extreme makeover," let me tell you. When I finally saw the Bible's truth about salvation, I discovered a joy and peace and assurance I had never known before. I will try to tell you what I learned in the chapters that follow. If you have been led to believe that your salvation depends on your own works, as I had been, I pray that you will experience the release the truth the Bible reveals can bring.

III

A DEVOUT CATHOLIC

Before going further, I want to take a few moments to explain why I am telling you all this. My prayer is that there will be people who will take it all in and discover the wonder of salvation as I did. My discovery of the biblical way of salvation forced a total review of everything I had been taught about salvation earlier. I was a person who could be called a devout Roman Catholic. I discovered that I was simply wrong about much of what I thought to be the way to heaven.

Now, let me say a few things about the Roman Catholic Church. First of all, I want to say that there are many things about the church that I deeply appreciate. I am grateful for its emphasis on the Trinity: there is one God who is Father, Son and Holy Spirit. I am grateful, too, that it takes a strong stand against many contemporary evils such as abortion, euthanasia and gay marriage.

There are also several aspects of their theology that I appreciate. Their latest catechism expresses a strong orthodoxy with regard to many elements of faith. In addition to their description of the divine Trinity, their steadfast affirmation of man as the image bearer of God needs to be stressed nowadays. But I finally had to face up to the fact that much of the Roman Catholic teaching regarding the way of salvation comes from sources outside the Bible. I began to realize that much of this teaching was a creation of man that could cause fatal confusion to those earnestly seeking salvation.

I represent the vast number of ordinary, lay members of the Roman Church who assumed much about the way of salvation that is not supported by the Bible. I believed my salvation depended on my receiving forgiveness of sins by a priest. I considered the door to the confessional booth the door to my salvation. Because I thought I could not enter heaven without a priest forgiving me, the door to the confessional became more important for my salvation than the cross of Calvary.

I also believed that Jesus died for the sins of the entire world. This meant that I could be forgiven, provided I received absolution of my sins by a priest. So I had the idea that Jesus did his part so that I could be saved, but I also had to do my part. I was taught that my baptism paid for what is called *original sin*, but after I came to what is called "the age of reason," every serious sin—the kind Rome calls *mortal sin*—must be confessed to a priest or I could go to hell. Because of these views, I could never have assurance of salvation. Roman Catholics cannot have that because there is always the chance that they will die before they have a chance to confess their latest mortal sins.

I believed that the good works I did, such as charitable acts, prayers to Mary and to other saints in heaven were very important because they please God and are instrumental in leading faithful people along the narrow path of salvation. I saw the good works I tried to do as being connected to salvation, even though I realized that they were not the primary source.

The primary source, I thought, was being forgiven by a priest, except in the case of what was called the "perfect contrition" that a person might express when a person who knew he was about to die was genuinely sorry for having offended God and there was no priest around to give the absolution required.

Yes, good works were very important to me as a Catholic. I believed that they were so pleasing to God that even though I continued to sin and went to confession week after week, because of good works, there was a good possibility that God would view me as a sufficiently good Roman Catholic to merit salvation. But if I would still have to spend a certain amount of time in purgatory for purification after my death, I figured that the good works I did would shorten my time there. When I was a Roman Catholic I believed that salvation is gained by faith in God plus good works plus confession of sins to a priest—you see: faith plus, plus. I never gave it a thought that it was possible for a believer to have a personal relationship with the Lord Jesus Christ. With his mother Mary, yes, and also with long-dead saints, but never with God. And so far as the Holy Spirit was concerned, I really never had a relation with him except to mention his name when I made the sign of the cross at prayer time. I would end prayers to Mary and other saints by saying, "In the name of the Father, the Son and the Holy Spirit," but I would have no idea what I was saying. That ritualistic saying meant nothing to me. It was merely a formality.

I didn't realize how much I had been misled by the church. Gradually, I discovered that the Bible's message was different from what I had been taught. And I discovered a new way of life. I became sure of my salvation, not because of anything I had done or would do, but exclusively because of what Christ had done. I learned what grace really was, and when I saw that, I realized that nothing I did could ever contribute to my salvation. The cross of Christ alone made my salvation possible. I was washed in the blood of the Lamb!

IV

THE WAY OF THE CROSS

As I mentioned earlier, I was fascinated to learn that the Apostle Paul spent time on the island of Malta—my ancestors came from that wind-swept place, and likely some of them had seen the water-logged, weather beaten apostle when he was tossed on their beach. (By the way, I am going to call him *Paul* from now on because that's the name he used during his missionary journeys.) But what really gripped me about this man was his conversion and his mighty work that followed. He became one of Christ's primary representatives on Planet Earth. And I made it my business to find out about the way of salvation as God described it through this mighty man.

I have always been interested in religion and assumed that whatever the Roman Church taught me was the truth. When I discovered that I was being short-changed by Catholicism, I not only felt betrayed, but also challenged to discover the real truth about the way of salvation. I am thankful that the television program God used to make me see that the way the Roman Church taught about salvation was false did not let me swing in the breeze but directed me to a local congregation of believers. Often people who are influenced by media religion do not realize their need of a true church if they are going to learn the truth of the Bible, and so they may move away from a church they learn is false into no church at all; often their second situation is as bad as their first. They give up on the church, begin to depend on their own intelligence and end up bitter and frustrated.

My wife Nicole and I were led to a Christian Reformed Church. I admit that the name *Christian Reformed* is puzzling; it was to us at first. There are actually several denominations that have the word *Reformed* in their names. These churches trace their origin back to the Protestant Reformation.

In the 16 Century, there was a great spiritual revival in Europe: many believers saw what I was beginning to see: that the Roman Catholic way of salvation was not biblical. Among these were the Lutherans, the Presbyterians, the Anabaptists and the Reformed. Well, Nicole and I went to a Reformed Church and this was very important for us.

It was important because it put us in touch with a centuries-long development of biblical teaching. For many years I was a reporter and columnist for the *Toronto Star,* and I learned, sometimes through bitter experience, that once people or institutions became adversaries, it was very difficult to discover the real truth. That is true in spades when it comes to religion.

There are many who are opposed to the Roman Catholic Church who become religious authorities for themselves. They just stay away from the church they grew up in and enjoy the freedom they have when they don't pay any attention to the church. People who do this put their souls in great danger.

When Nicole and I became members of a church that was part of the 16th Century Reformation tradition, I learned how thousands of people who rejected the Roman Catholic way of salvation did not reject what is often called the *holy catholic church.* Notice, I did not write "Roman Catholic Church," but holy catholic church. There's a big difference. Actually the word *catholic* means universal—something that exists throughout the entire world and throughout the centuries. So the word *catholic* refers to those who have believed in Christ for centuries all over the world. The church we now attend takes the long history and worldwide extent of Christ's Church seriously, and that is why we often declare that we believe in "a holy catholic church." We are part of that great church. And within our local church, we rejoice as the biblical way of salvation is proclaimed to us. That way is the way of the cross.

I want to tell others about what I discovered so that they, too, will experience the joy and relief I did when I learned that my salvation did not depend on me but solely on Christ's finished work. If you stay with me, you will discover that salvation is not through the elaborate system the Roman Church presents, but salvation is through faith alone. As soon as we add all sorts of rules and conditions to the way of salvation, we deny the way Christ's cross takes away the sin of all those who believe in this Savior. We cannot have it both ways: either salvation is through God's finished work on the cross or it is through our works.

The great message that comes into our lives when we read the Bible and attend a church that exalts the Bible is that we are freed from the obligation of accumulating our own merit to pay for our salvation. How can people come to this faith?

They can come to it by believing the message of the Bible. As the apostle puts it in the New Testament book of Romans, "Faith comes from hearing the message, and the message is heard through the word of God." (10:17)

One of the main reasons that the Roman Catholic teaching attaches so many conditions to salvation is that it is a church that is built on the Bible and tradition. It is a "Bible plus" religion. When we take the Bible and the Bible alone as the foundation of our faith, we discover that God has provided for man's salvation through Christ's shed blood. This is a major theme that runs through the entire Bible. The Old Testament is the foundation upon which the New Testament is built, and when we take the two together, we learn that there is no salvation without the shedding of blood, and the blood that has been shed is Jesus' blood. That blood was enough to save anyone who flees to Christ and believes that he is Savior and Lord.

TWO MEN FROM MALTA

When Jesus of Nazareth lived a perfectly obedient life and died on the hill called Golgotha, he accomplished a perfect salvation that no human being could ever accomplish; he did for sinners what they could never do for themselves. When God became man in Jesus Christ, that perfect man, who was also God, became the person who paid for human sin in a sacrifice that needs never be repeated. Christ's once and for all payment of himself on the cross needs never to be repeated, just as, once you've paid last month's rent, you don't have to pay it again. And it needs nothing additional to make it effective. Jesus' sacrifice became exactly what was needed to free believers from their bondage to sin.

But people like us always prefer to do things for ourselves. Nowhere is this truer than in salvation. We want to help God save us. This is why we always want to supplement Christ's work with our good works. But no— salvation is a gift. It comes into our lives through grace and grace alone. Grace, as you know, is something that comes into our lives freely—it's just there, and all we can do is say "Thank you."

The apostle Paul put it this way: "For it is by grace that you have been saved, through faith—and this is not from yourselves, it is the gift of God, not by works, so that no one can boast." (Ephesians 2:8)

The great 16th Century reformer, Martin Luther lived in anguish until he discovered that salvation was by grace alone, apart from works. He was a super-scrupulous Augustinian monk who realized that his sins were great enough to condemn him to hell. Try as he might, he could not do enough good works to give him certainty of salvation. He was sure he was going to go to hell. And then, one day, he discovered the truth of the gospel of salvation by grace alone.

As an Augustinian monk, Luther had studied Psalms, Romans and Galatians, three important Bible books, and had lectured on them in the Seminary. He was a brilliant scholar. And as he studied, he became more and more sure that he could not do anything for his own salvation. Then one day, he suddenly understood Romans 1:16-17 where the apostle Paul wrote: "I am not ashamed of the gospel, because it is the power of God for the salvation of everyone who believes: first for the Jew, then for the Gentile. For in the gospel a righteousness from God is revealed, a righteousness that is by faith from first to last...."

Luther saw that the righteousness he had been trying to achieve for himself had to be set aside for what Romans 1:17 calls *the righteousness of God.* That righteousness is actually the righteousness that God himself made a reality when he offered his one and only Son as an offering for human sin. Now, whoever believes in that Son—Jesus—has Jesus' righteousness given to him. Jesus paid it all; believers do not have to pay anything for their own salvation.

Once Luther saw that he didn't have to pay for his own sins because Jesus Christ already had, he earnestly called others to believe only in Christ for their salvation. He explained that any works that we do are unacceptable to the holy God because they are imperfect and contaminated. Salvation is possible only because of the blood of Jesus. All of us are condemned by nature and all of us desperately need a Savior. Jesus is the Savior. We cannot possibly save ourselves. God tells us: "Don't even try."

When I was going to catechism, no one ever told me that Jesus had died in my place on the cross. I simply saw the biblical record of Jesus' execution as a terribly sad ending to the story of his life. What upset me the most was that his followers did nothing to try to rescue Jesus or halt his execution. Even though I knew about Jesus' death on the cross, I knew nothing whatsoever about the Bible, so I didn't have the slightest idea about what his death meant for me.

If I had been taught the Bible, I would have had an entirely different view of Jesus' sacrifice. I would have learned the powerful message of the Old Testament that tells how bulls, goats and sheep had to be slaughtered as sin offerings so that the people of Israel would not be destroyed. Literally hundreds of thousands of these animals were slaughtered and their blood was sprinkled on the altar and sometimes on the ark of the covenant in order that the people of Israel would know that the "wages of sin is death." (Romans 6:23)

They had to realize that, because they sinned against God, they were liable to receive the death sentence. Already in the Old Testament, God stepped in with his mercy and accepted the sacrifices they brought him as payment for their sins. But, of course, these animal sacrifices could never take away their sins. "It is impossible for the blood of bulls and goats to take away sins." (Hebrews 10:4) Those Old Testament sacrifices were provisional, temporary sacrifices that pointed forward to the perfect sacrifice that Jesus was going to bring.

If I would have been taught the Bible when I was a boy, I would have learned that all that blood shed during the Old Testament times made clear that all of us human beings are in a terrible predicament. There is only one way that we can be saved and that is through shed blood. But our own blood can't do it because our blood is the blood of imperfect people. Only someone who is sinless and perfect can save us.

And so it was that after more than 1600 years of animal sacrifices, God finally sent his precious Son into our world to become the "Lamb of God who takes away the sin of the world." (John 1:29) The eternal God entered our world of time and space, and in the person of Christ Jesus, who is the Second Person of the Holy Trinity, took our sins upon himself and suffered, bled and died to pay our debt. As Paul puts it: "God made him who had no sin to be sin for us, so that in him we might become the righteousness of God." (2 Corinthians 5:21) That's what Christ did when he died on Calvary's cross. Can anyone imagine a salvation greater than this? Only God would think of such a salvation and only God could carry it through to completion.

As I became more familiar with the Bible I discovered that this great salvation could be mine if I believed in Jesus as my Savior. Sinful human beings are saved when they believe the blessed good news of salvation through God's sacrifice of his Son. We must confess that we are depraved and helpless by nature, guilty of rebellion against God's law and doomed to condemnation. By nature, we are doomed to experience the eternal death that is eternal separation from God—and that is hell. That's the bad news.

But the good news is that if we believe in Jesus and his finished work on the cross, our sins are completely blotted out. Those who believe are no longer enemies of God but they are reconciled to him because when God looks at them he sees them clothed in Jesus' righteousness. He looks at us as if we have been entirely obedient. He justifies us because of the finished work of Jesus. He considers us just: it is *just as if we had never sinned.*

My good friend from Malta, Paul the apostle, put it this way: "But now he has reconciled you by Christ's physical body through death to present you holy in his sight, without blemish and free from accusation. (Colossians 1:22)

As I have said, as a young boy, a catechumen, I was never given the slightest hint that salvation becomes ours solely through faith in the Lord Jesus Christ. Not one church functionary told me that all I had to do was anchor my hope in Christ's haven of rest. No one did this because it has long been the Roman Church's position that salvation is achieved by human beings through a combination of faith plus works.

Because the "faith plus works" formula has been the conventional wisdom for so many years among so many people, the average person doesn't ever really think about God's real plan for salvation. Most of us do not really begin to understand the seriousness of sin; we consider it quite normal to rebel against God. Most people do not realize that God so abhors sin that only the perfectly innocent Christ Jesus could rescue sinful people through the shedding of his blood—his sacrifice alone can remove the curse that has befallen us. He rescued us by voluntarily taking our guilt upon himself and going to the cross in our place.

And let me say this as well: when Christ was crucified, the visible side of what happened was a very small part of what he actually did to save us. Remember, when Jesus was crucified there were three hours of darkness, and during that time, Jesus of Nazareth drank the cup of God's wrath against the sin of the world. God poured out that wrath on his only Son. Oh, there is a mystery here that must leave us speechless! Amazing grace!

All this staggers the mind. The Bible makes very clear that much more occurred when Jesus was crucified than the driving of nails into his hands and feet. Jesus was enduring the curse that rests on sinners. The Bible tells us that anyone who hangs on a tree is under divine curse. Look at this: "If a man guilty of a capital offense is put to death and his body is hung on a tree, you must not leave his body on the tree overnight. Be sure to bury him that same day, because anyone who is hung on a tree is under God's curse. You must not desecrate the land the LORD your God is giving you as an inheritance." (Deuteronomy 21:22-23)

We know that Jesus recoiled as he thought of his coming torture and death on the cross. But the depth of his agony when he contemplated the cross was not caused by the ordinary physical side of the suffering he would endure. Jesus was well aware of the customary cruelties of the Romans: countless were crucified before him, others were torn apart in Rome's Coliseum, some where cast into boiling water, sawed in half, burned at the stake or thrown into a fiery pit. As an atrocious death, Jesus' death was no different from these. But as Jesus approached the cross, he was given a clarity of vision that allowed him to see that what he would endure would so transcend all these atrocities it could not be compared to them: the sinless Christ would be saturated in our depravity and would receive the full force of God's wrath unleashed against human wickedness.

Is it any wonder that he sweat drops of blood in the Garden of Gethsemane when he considered that he would receive the wrath of God against all human wickedness, murder, rape, robbery, hate, genocide and every other evil act committed since the fall of man into sin until human history ends with Christ's return? No wonder he cried out: "Father, if you are willing, take this cup from me; yet not my will, but yours be done." (Luke 22:42)

Nobody ever told me about this as I was growing up; I just figured that if I were going to be saved, I would have to do it myself. But no! Jesus saved me.

Actually the Father and the Son and the Holy Spirit saved me. God who loved his Son more than any human being can ever love a son determined to make his Son the offering for sin. God cannot ignore sin. Sin must be punished. Rather than leave it unpunished, he punished it by pouring out his wrath on his Son, and his Son agreed—he was totally obedient to his Father's will. And the Holy Spirit was there every moment of Jesus' life and during his sacrifice, empowering and supporting him. God laid the punishment of our sin on his Son. This means that God took our punishment upon himself when he punished his Son.

Yes, the Bible makes this very clear, and if we had been taught the Bible as children, we would have known it. Six or seven hundred years before Jesus was crucified, speaking in the power of the Holy Spirit, the Old Testament prophet Isaiah spoke of what God would do. "We all, like sheep, have gone astray, each of us has turned to his own way; and the Lord has laid on him the iniquity of us all. (Isaiah 53:6)

When the Father poured out his wrath on his Son, Jesus experienced the horrors of hell. In the horror of the three-hour darkness we have mentioned, the Son experienced separation from his Father. "He became sin for us," as we have seen (2 Corinthians 5:21), and so our sin was punished when Jesus tasted the bitter cup of abandonment by his Father; the very love-bond of the Holy Trinity was briefly shattered.

"And at the ninth hour Jesus cried out in a loud voice, "Eloi, Eloi, lama sabachthani?"—which means, "My God, my God, why have you forsaken me?" (Mark 15:34)

The people of Israel should not have been surprised by this because fourteen hundred years earlier God had given them the Passover. At the center of the Passover, there was the unblemished lamb that was slain for the peoples' sin. Centuries before the cross, God's people learned that God's justice demanded that sin would be paid for. Way back then God established the principle of substitution—the lamb substituted for the people who should have been destroyed.

The Bible puts it this way (this is God speaking): "On that same night I will pass through Egypt and strike down every firstborn—both men and animals—and I will bring judgment on all the gods of Egypt. I am the Lord. The blood will be a sign for you on the houses where you are; and when I see the blood, I will pass over you. No destructive plague will touch you when I strike Egypt." (Exodus 121:12-13)

Jesus the Lamb of God is my substitute. No one ever told me about this when I was growing up. So I foolishly went about trying to earn my own salvation with my measly works. Now I know that the obedience of Christ has become my obedience and I am protected from God's wrath.

But there is more. I have been grafted into Christ and I have become part of the family of God. When we believe in Christ, we become brothers and sisters of Jesus and joint heirs with Christ of heaven's glory.

Our salvation is assured.

No condemnation now I dread,
For Christ, and all in him is mine!
Alive in Him, my living Head,
and clothed in righteousness divine,
bold I approach the eternal Throne
and claim the crown, through Christ, my own.
(And Can it Be? – Charles Wesley)

V

SAVED BY FAITH

When I discovered that the way of salvation differed from what the Roman Church had taught me, I learned that I was saved by faith alone, not faith plus works. Please do not misunderstand: the faith that saves is a faith that works; in other words a person who has true, saving faith will exhibit the reality of his faith in a renewed life. If a person has faith and continues to live the way Satan wants him to and never shows any interest in the things of the Lord, whatever faith such a person has is not true, saving faith. A life of good works flows from saving faith. But salvation has nothing whatsoever to do with our works; it has everything to do with our faith. If our works were part of the salvation equation, we would be eternally lost because every work we do is imperfect.

The Old Testament prophet Isaiah is very blunt about this. He writes: "All of us have become like one who is unclean, and all our righteous acts are like filthy rags; we all shrivel up like a leaf, and like the wind our sins sweep us away. (Isaiah 64:6) The Apostle Paul affirmed this Old Testament teaching about human sinfulness by quoting Psalms 53:1-3 and declaring: "There is no one righteous, not even one; there is no one who understands, no one who seeks God. All have turned away, they have together become worthless; there is no one who does good not even one." (Romans 3:10-11) And when he talked that way, he did not consider himself exempt from this corruption. He bemoaned his natural tendency to sin against God when he cried out: "What I do is not the good I want to do; no, the evil I do not want to do—this I keep on doing. ...What a wretched man I am! Who will rescue me from this body of death? Thanks be to God—through Jesus Christ our Lord!" (Romans 7: 19,24)

The Bible tells us that each one of us is sinful from conception. In Psalm 51:5, David, the great king of Israel, declared, "Surely I was sinful at birth, sinful from the time my mother conceived me." We do not become sinful several months after birth when we begin to be naughty; no, our sin is a birth defect—we are born sinful. The disobedience of our first parents in the Garden of Eden guaranteed that every child born entered the world as a guilty sinner. But not only are we born guilty, our every human faculty has been so corrupted by sin that it is not capable of pleasing God. When I speak of our faculties, I mean our will, our emotions and our intellect. Our will has been seriously injured by the Fall, our emotions have become unreliable and our minds have become incapable of thinking clearly about God.

When I turned away from the teaching of the Roman Church, I had to give up the idea that any of my works contribute to my salvation. Roman Catholic teaching recognizes the man's fall into sin was a damaging calamity, but it does not go so far as to say that we are now incapable of doing any good that might contribute to our salvation. In its latest catechism, it states: "Original sin does not have the character of a personal fault in any of Adam's descendants. It is a deprivation of original holiness and justice, but human nature has not been totally corrupted...." (Section 405) The Roman Catholic Church believes that human reason has remained capable of knowing much about God, and that man's will is still sufficiently free to enable a person to find his way back to God. Original sin, in Roman Catholicism, is mainly guilt; it is not a corruption that renders us without any resources for contributing to our salvation.

At the time of the Protestant Reformation, the reformers, following the lead of a prominent fifth century theologian, St. Augustine, declared that every element of our nature has been so corrupted by the fall that we are unable to find our way to God so that we can be saved. The Roman catechism describes the position of the Reformers this way: "The first Protestant Reformers, on the contrary, taught that original sin has radically perverted man and destroyed his freedom; they identified the sin inherited by each man with the tendency to evil, which would be insurmountable." (Section 406)

Excuse me for this historical tour, but it's very important to understand that everything in a church's theology depends on how the church describes the effect of the Fall on human nature. A church that says that the Fall was very serious but not totally incapacitating, can go on to say that those who have been affected by the Fall are still able to do some good. They are able to make the first turn toward God, and then, if they use their natures to cooperate with God's grace, they can create an accumulation of good works they can turn in later as partial payment for their sins. This is the way the Roman Catholic Church reasons. The Protestant Reformers, however, saw that the way the Bible describes the impact of the Fall on human nature leaves us with no possibility of turning to God and no possibility of creating a single good work that we can turn in as payment for our sins.

Have you ever wondered why the Roman Catholic Church is the largest Christian denomination in the world? It's extremely impressive isn't it? When I was a Roman Catholic I assumed that a church that had so many members must be the one, true church. No one can blame me for believing that what the church taught me was true. I was one of hundreds of millions of people worldwide who assume this.

It is very likely true that the reason that the Roman Church is as big as it is, is that it tells its followers that they are not completely helpless when it comes to doing something for their salvation. The idea that the Fall was serious but it did not leave us totally incapable of obeying God and paying for our own sins plays right into the way we like to think of ourselves.

We travel along, thinking that we have free will that is capable of turning to the Lord any time we want to, we have pretty good heads so we can think about God, and every once in a while we feel a religious emotion sweep over our hearts. Our egos tell us that we are not so bad, and God should be pleased with us if we go to church occasionally and pray certain prescribed prayers and maybe even read the Bible a couple of times a year. Besides, we sometimes feel constrained to help the poor and maybe even fight against one of the glaring social ills like abortion. Put all this together and you have a pretty good person, not the best perhaps, but as good as many and better than some. All these good things about ourselves makes up a package that has some value in making up with God for our sin - that's what we tend to think.

We fail to see that we are deceiving ourselves when we think the way Rome teaches people to think. The Old Testament prophet Jeremiah wrote, "The heart is deceitful above all things and beyond cure. Who can understand it?" (Jeremiah 17:3) A church whose teachings appeal to our deceitful hearts has a good formula for success. But, sad to say, it does not have a good formula for salvation.

When I left the Roman Church and became involved in a church that proclaimed biblical truth, I discovered what a helpless sinner I was. I discovered that if I were going to be saved, everything about my salvation would have to come from God. Everything. What is there in the Bible that can bring a proud man like me, who had long thought that God was sufficiently pleased with my devotion to virtually assure me of eternal life—what could ever bring me to my senses? Two things.

The first one was the Law of God.

The apostle Paul knew all about the Law of God. The religious sect he was a member of—the Pharisees—made the Law of God the center of its life.

When Pharisees talked about the Law of God, they talked about the Ten Commandments, the other laws we find in the Old Testament, and more than six hundred other laws that they had made up themselves. They fine-tuned the law, they tweaked the law, they talked about the law, and, above all, they thought they kept it meticulously. They looked down their noses at everybody else. And Jesus made very clear, while he was here, that they were going to burn in hell because of the way they thought and acted. Just read Matthew 23, if you want to see how Jesus rejected the Pharisee's way of thinking and told them that they would be highly uncomfortable in the place they were going.

Paul's buddies, the Pharisees, could get away with their way of handling the law because they made it an external matter. The law said, "Don't kill," they didn't kill. (They might get someone else to do it for them, but they didn't do it themselves.) Right on down the line, they could read off the Ten Commandments (Exodus 20:1-17) and announce: "No problem—we keep them perfectly."

Then Jesus came and he announced that the law was about the heart; it had to do with inner feelings and attitudes. Jesus said that the commandment against murder was about loving your neighbors and helping them. He said that the commandment against adultery was about lusting after any woman you weren't married to.

So it was that when the Apostle Paul talked about the law in Romans 3:20 he said: "No one will be declared righteous in [God's] sight by observing the law; rather, through the law we become conscious of sin." In other words, when we understand the law of God, we see the depth of our sin.

Using words of the Old Testament, Jesus summarized the law in a way that reveals how impossible it is for us to keep it. He said, "Love the Lord your God with all your heart and with all your soul and with all your mind.' This is the first and greatest commandment. And the second is like it: 'Love your neighbor as yourself.' All the law and the prophets hang on these two commandments." (Matthew 22:37-40)

When we look at the law the way Jesus did and realize that it's about love—love for God and love for our neighbor—we realize that we don't measure up. When I did that, I realized I was a wretched sinner. You see, the law shows us how deeply the Fall of man into sin has affected us. We are corrupt, we are contaminated, we are powerless to do anything that can please God.

But there is more in the Bible that enables us sinners to see just how dreadfully, hopelessly sinful we are. The second thing that brought me to my senses and enabled me to see the depths of my sin is found in the New Testament. It is the cross.

Yes, the law can show us our sin, but the cross is able to show us our sin even more effectively. When we measure our lives by the law, we use information that has been written down—the Ten Commandments were written by the finger of God on two stone tablets, and the rest of the law is scattered through the first five books of the Bible. We read about Christ's death on the Bible's pages, too, but with the crucifixion, the event itself shatters our pride and crushes us. We are overwhelmed as we see that we are guilty of supreme rebellion against heaven.

If ever there was a blood-stained book, it is the Bible. The Old Testament runs heavy with the blood of countless animals slain by the priests for the sins of God's people. The slaughter never ended because the sacrifices were inherently incapable of paying for human sin and because the magnitude of human sin was so great it could never be paid for. The ghastly sacrificial work of the priests who butchered the animals and carefully separated the body parts, eating some, burning others, often sprinkling the blood on the altar, pointed forward to the sacrifice of infinite worth, the sacrifice of God in the flesh, Jesus of Nazareth.

When I read the Bible for myself and listened to preaching and teaching that was centered on the Bible, I began to see the magnitude of my sin as I grasped the significance of Christ's sacrificial death. I saw something different from what I had seen when I looked at the paintings and images and the crucifix that formed Roman Catholic piety. I began to see that the cross pointed to a suffering more horrible than these pictures and images could ever depict.

After the Protestant Reformation, the Roman Catholic Church stressed the physical suffering of Christ with high fervor. This was done to counter the Reformation emphasis on the meaning of Christ's suffering, while rejecting images and paintings that centered on flagellation, the thorn-crown and the nails and spear of the crucifixion itself. This emphasis on the physical side of Christ's death reached a high point in Mel Gibson's film *The Passion of Christ*, which relied largely on the Post-Reformation excesses in stressing Christ's physical suffering, especially the writings of the 19th Century nun/author Sister Anne Catherine Emmerich. As a devout Catholic, my thoughts about the cross were formed by these visualizations. The crucifix, of course, depicts Jesus on the cross.

As I gradually outgrew my Roman Catholic way of thinking, I began to understand the meaning of the cross differently. Whereas before I had thought of it as an unfortunate ending to an otherwise successful life, I began to realize that the cross was the last, great battle between God and Satan, a battle that ended in Christ's victory, and my salvation depended entirely on that victory. Yes, I had occasionally been moved to tears as I contemplated the intensity of Jesus' physical agony, but I never realized that Christ had paid for all my sin, there on the cross. I always assumed that he had done his part and now I was obligated to do mine.

The cross has become the center of my faith because I now see it as the supreme revelation of the depth of my sin and the supreme revelation of the infinite love of God. I saw this, too, in the writings of the Apostle Paul. His letters, which dominate the New Testament, admit the apparent absurdity of God's making everything about salvation depend on the cross. He concedes that the very idea of the cross being the centerpiece for salvation is an affront to both Jews and Gentiles. Nothing could offend Jews more than the idea that God died on a cross, and the sophisticated Greeks had nothing in their mythologies that came anywhere near this—for them the cross was foolishness!

One gets the impression that for the Apostle Paul, the cross was both an offense and foolishness before his conversion. As a Jew it offended him and as a learned man it made no sense to him at all. But the Spirit of the living Savior revealed its glorious importance to him, and he became the great apostle of the cross.

The cross enables us to sense how great our sin is—it provides us with a measure of our sin that we are incapable of fathoming, but it is a measure nonetheless. Being sinners as we are, the very sin that we acknowledge prohibits us from understanding how great our sin is. We are skilled at finding excuses for our sin. We lie to ourselves about why we sin and we succeed in deceiving ourselves. We justify ourselves. When we compare ourselves to others we invariably come out the winners. Our sin keeps us from seeing how great our sin is. This is a vicious reality, but reality it most certainly is.

This is where the cross helps us. When we look beyond the obvious physical aspects of the crucifixion and remember that most of the time Jesus was on the cross the entire scene was obscured by a divinely arranged darkness, we begin to realize that what happened at Golgotha was a terrifying transaction within the depths of the Trinity. It was at the cross that Christ satisfied the ethical demands that were rooted in God's perfect righteousness. It was there that the wrath of God against human sin was poured out and the Second Person of the Trinity, incarnate in the flesh as Jesus of Nazareth, absorbed that wrath.

I learned a word I had never heard before; unfortunately it is not even found in most modern translations. But a recent biblical translation, the English Standard Version, uses it where it should be used. It is the word *propitiation*. Look at this from 1 John 4:10. "In this is love, not that we have loved God but that he loved us and sent his Son to be the propitiation for our sins." The word *propitiation* captures what happened when the Son of God gave himself in sacrifice on the cross. He paid for sin.

Three years earlier, John the Baptist had called out, when he saw Jesus approach: "Look, the Lamb of God who takes away the sin of the world." (John 1:29) Jesus takes away human sin. We cannot do that. Our sin is too great and our works too feeble and corrupt. The very idea that we might be able to do something for our own salvation indicates that we understand neither the depths of our predicament nor our total inability to do anything about it.

I began to understand that the way of salvation Rome presents contradicts the central teaching of the Word of God. This is very difficult to see because of the heavy religious trappings and impressive ritual that are part of Roman Catholicism. But when you strip away all the layers of the onion and come to the heart or the matter you discover that, with Rome, works are the heart of the matter. To be sure, they are works plus grace, true enough, but with Rome salvation is not by grace alone. The Bible, though, says that salvation is by grace alone. Because Rome compromises this biblical teaching, it is disqualified as a teacher of salvation.

This is a serious deformation of religion. It is, in fact, the most serious deformation of biblical religion there could possibly be. What is this?

Well, my good friend who made an unexpected visit to Malta many years ago—the Apostle Paul—wrote the book of Galatians in the Bible to show why it is dreadfully wrong to include human works in the achievement of salvation. Galatians is his angriest book. He was so upset with the people he wrote to that he said that anyone who believed as they did was anathema, and if you grew up in the Roman

Catholic Church as I did, you know what the word anathema means. *Anathema* means "condemned to hell." Paul said that if they did not correct their thinking about salvation, their souls would be in jeopardy.

And what was their problem?

It was this: he had brought them the gospel of salvation by grace alone clearly and unmistakably. He explained to them that no man can be saved by observing the law; we can be saved only through faith in Jesus Christ. Jesus paid it all; we pay not a penny. But the Galatian Christians started to listen to representatives of the Jewish faith (they were likely Jewish Christians) who said that, yes Christ had done a lot for our salvation, but the Galatian Christians should also receive the sign of Old Testament religion, the sign of circumcision. If they received the covenant sign of Old Testament religion their religion would be complete. Paul was appalled. If they received the sign of circumcision, they obligated themselves to keep the entire law of God. If they did that, they would be mixing what must never be mixed: they would be saying they were saved through the cross and saved through their own works.

In other words, the Galatian Christians wanted to mix the work of Christ with their own works. They said that salvation comes from believing in Christ plus keeping the law.

Paul was horrified. He was scandalized. He spoke to them as sharply as he did because he realized that as soon as you include works in the salvation equation, you show that you don't understand the cross. As Paul put it: "if righteousness could be gained through the law, Christ died for nothing!" (Galatians 2:21)

Now, as you know there are all sorts of religious errors. There is no form of Christianity that is without error. But there are different degrees of seriousness when it comes to error. Some are relatively minor. But the error that says that we are saved by Christ's sacrifice plus our works is the worst of all because it reveals a fundamental misunderstanding of the cross of Christ. This error declares that Christ's infinitely valuable sacrifice was not enough to save us: something had to be added to it, and we are the ones who must supply that something.

The heart of the gospel is that "God so loved the world that he gave his only begotten Son that whoever believes in him will not perish but have everlasting life." (John 3:16) The most serious religious error is tampering with the heart of the gospel. We may not say: God so loved the world that he gave his only begotten Son so that whoever believes in him and does good works will not perish but have everlasting life. To say this is to destroy what God in his love and mercy has created for us poor sinners: salvation by grace alone.

It is to say that Christ died for nothing! No one may say that. No church may say that, no matter how big it may be, no matter how impressive its traditions are, no matter how many people follow its teachings. The Roman Catholic Church may not give its members the impression that they will be saved if they do what the church tells them to do. Surely, their teachings emphasize the importance of Christ's death, but they also deny that Christ's death and his death alone can save us. Nothing else can.

Saving Faith

Now then, if it is true that only Christ's sacrifice on the cross can save us, the question is: how can we benefit from what Christ has accomplished at Calvary? After all, Jesus was crucified about 2,000 years ago; he was crucified not we. How can what happened when he died affect us today? This is where saving faith comes into the picture. Saving faith connects believers with Christ so that his sin-payment becomes their sin-payment.

Before going further, it is necessary to describe saving faith. As we all know, the word *faith* refers to a broad range of feelings. Sometimes it means *self-confidence;* as in the sentence: "I have faith that I will succeed." Sometimes *faith* refers to the belief that various events occurred; for example, a person might say that he believes that Jesus of Nazareth actually lived in Israel 2,000 years ago. Sometimes it means that a person believes that certain miracles occurred; for example, a person may say that he believes that Christ rose from the dead. Such forms of faith are good, but they are not actually saving faith because they do not connect the believer with the living Christ so that what Christ has done is applied to the person who believes.

Here is a description of saving faith that was written about the same time great numbers of people turned away from Roman Catholic teaching because they realized that that teaching was not supported by the Bible. When you read this description of saving faith, you will notice that it is a conviction that the infinite price that Christ paid for human sin has been applied to me personally and, therefore, I may be confident that I will never have to pay for my sins.

The Heidelberg Catechism, written in 1563, just 46 years after Martin Luther nailed the 95 statements that started the Protestant Reformation, answers the question *What is true faith?* this way: "True faith is not only the certain knowledge whereby I hold for truth all that God has revealed to us in his Word, but also an assured confidence, which the Holy Spirit works by the gospel in my heart, that not only to others, but to me also, remission of sin, everlasting righteousness and salvation are freely given by God, merely of grace, only for the sake of Christ's merits."

This description of true, saving, faith reflects the biblical description of salvation as that which occurs without reference to our works. Our works have nothing whatsoever to do with our being saved. In the Bible, the book of Ephesians says this plainly in chapter 2:8-9: "For it is by grace you have been saved, through faith—and this not from yourselves, it is the gift of God—not by works, so that no one can boast."

The catechism we were looking at declares that believers are saved, "merely of grace, only for the sake of Christ's merits." Exactly. Ephesians 2:8-9 declares that salvation is of grace, through faith, not by works. This contradicts the way the Roman Catholic Church taught me that I had to complete a certain amount of good works to pay for my sins. Jesus paid a part of my bill, but I will have to pay the rest of it. Not true, the Bible says: Jesus paid it all. Your bill has been stamped paid and, if you died within the next 47 seconds, without a chance to confess your sins, you would be saved. And the price has been paid only through the work of Christ, not through our work.

Surely, this is the meaning of Ephesians' strong affirmation to believers: *you have been saved, not from yourselves, it is a divine gift, not of works, so that no one can boast.* Interestingly, this affirmation is made so that no saved person can ever boast. We would be able to boast if we contributed to our own salvation in any way, no matter how slight. To be sure, we might recognize that our works were a minor element in making our salvation possible, but, even so, however minor, if we had anything whatsoever to do with our own salvation, we would boast.

It was a great discovery for me to find out that I was saved, not by works, but by faith alone. But I would like to say that this discovery was not just an intellectual discovery. True Christianity is not like doing a multiple choice test that includes the question "What is saving faith"? with this as one of the answers: *saving faith is believing the truth of the gospel, being assured by the Holy Spirit that my sins are paid for and knowing that my salvation is by grace alone.* I did not check off the correct answer and say hallelujah. No. This saving faith had a powerful impact on my life. It changed me inside. It made me a new creature in Christ. It connected me to Christ. It made my very experience of life totally different from what it was before. Saving faith fills a person with joy because it transforms him from the inside out.

When I was a Roman Catholic, my religious life consisted in a determined effort to make sure that I covered all the bases so that I would be saved when death struck. Being a good Christian involved a program, going to confession, going to mass, being forgiven by a priest, praying to Mary and a couple of my favorite saints. That was the life of faith for me. That's what happens when you are led to believe that your salvation depends on your meeting the requirements for salvation. You find out what you have to do and you do it, like a good catechumen, and later, like a good man, like a good woman.

When I became a true believer, being a Christian became a totally different experience for me. You see, saving faith does not come into a person's life at the end of an intellectual exercise. Saving faith is a special creation of God's Holy Spirit in the heart of a believer. The blinding realization that you can do nothing to save yourself and the overwhelming joy that comes when you learn that God has done everything to make your salvation sure, is something that God creates inside of you.

One of the most striking descriptions of the way believers are transformed by the Holy Spirit is found in the book that Paul wrote to the church in Ephesus. After describing the great work of salvation God has accomplished in Christ, Paul wrote: "And you also were included in Christ when you heard the word of truth, the gospel of your salvation. Having, believed, you were marked in him with a seal, the promised Holy Spirit, who is a deposit guaranteeing our inheritance until the redemption of those who are God's possession—to the praise of his glory." (Ephesians 1:13-14)

If you didn't understand that material from Ephesians fully, don't panic. It's hard to grasp in its fullness. But notice this: what you just read says that believers are sealed with the promised Holy Spirit who is deposited within them. True saving faith is a heavenly reality that is implanted in the heart of a true believer. There is no comparison between true saving faith that recognizes that God takes care of everything when it comes to salvation and a form of faith that enlists us in a program in which we have to get busy and take care of what's been assigned us in the salvation program. True saving faith is a new creation of God in the heart of a believer.

You see, true saving faith in Christ as the only Savior who takes care of everything for us actually unites us to Christ. The Apostle Paul described how this true, saving faith did this for him to the point where he could say that he had been crucified with Christ. Look at this from Galatians 2:20—"I have been crucified with Christ and I no longer live, but Christ lives in me. The life I live in the body, I live by faith in the Son of God, who loved me and gave himself for me."

The faith that saves cannot be described as an intellectual reality, though it has an intellectual element. It is more than intellectual. It is a spiritual reality that affects the deepest levels of a human personality. What I believe about Christ now is very different from what I used to believe about him. I used to believe certain facts about him that I considered true. But now my faith connects me with Christ.

In Romans 6, the Apostle tells how he is united with Christ in his death and his resurrection. In verse 8 he speaks of having died with Christ and having been raised with Christ. For him faith was a power that transformed him because it connected him with Jesus Christ. He did not simply believe certain facts about Christ were true, but he knew he was connected to Christ by the power of the Holy Spirit.

This, as you can see, is a totally different experience from what I had when I was a Roman Catholic, plodding along in my spiritual life, doing what the priest told me to do. I didn't feel close to Christ at all. Christ Jesus was too exalted for a common person like me to have a personal relationship with him. I was grateful that there was a group of common, ordinary people called saints that I could relate to. I related to Jesus' mother, and to some of the other saints. But not to Christ. Oh, I prayed to Jesus now and then but he was somewhat distant.

I figured that someday I would see him, after I had done my purgatory time and collected some merit of my own, but the very idea of having Christ within me and living in the power of Christ's Spirit was totally foreign to me. Yes, we are saved by faith alone, not of works. And the faith that saves us is placed within us by God's Spirit. The Fall of man into sin has caused damage so devastating, there is no way we can make our way to God—our heads aren't good enough, our emotions aren't good enough, and our will is a wimp. God and God alone gives the faith that saves us. That's good news because if God didn't give that faith no one would be saved. But this news is also upsetting. If it is true, how can an ordinary human being ever be saved? What determines whether or not any of us will be saved?

If faith is a gift, who gets the gift? I thought about that a lot. And when I found the answer, I was humbled and grateful and overwhelmed all at the same time. To answer the question we have to look at a word a lot of people know little or nothing of. I didn't. It's the word that's the title of the next chapter.

VI

PREDESTINATION

Let me just review some of the major ideas that we have been looking at in order to see where I had to go to discover how the way of salvation by grace works on the deepest level. I guess the most fundamental lesson I had to learn when I discovered the wonder of salvation by grace alone, through faith, was that my works had nothing to do with my salvation.

Salvation requires a payment for my sin so enormous, I could not even begin to nibble away at the edges of it. In fact, the payment it requires is of a kind that I could never provide. Trying to pay the cost of my salvation would be like trying to pay off the six trillion dollar national debt of the United States with Indonesian currency.

This contradicted the impression I had been given by the Roman Church that my salvation could be secured by my following a way the church laid out for me. I believed that if I confessed my sins to a priest and he absolved me, I was in the clear. In other words my thoughts and actions were taken up into the process of salvation. To be sure, I knew that the sacrifice of Christ on the cross was necessary; in fact, it was so necessary that it must be offered up again and again at daily Mass. My attendance at mass assured me that bits of Christ's merit would be added to my account. But I was also given the impression that I had better work hard at accumulating some merit of my own. If I didn't I would spend a lot of time in purgatory, or possibly miss out on heaven altogether.

Sometimes the Roman Catholic teaching regarding salvation is described as *analytic.* Let me explain. When we want to know what is in of a bowl of pudding (just to take an example), we analyze the substances that make it up. Well, Catholics believe that when God checks a person over to see if that person is worthy of salvation, he analyzes the person. God looks at the person's record, what he has failed to do and what he has done. He checks if the person believes the facts of Christ's life. He checks off how often he has gone to confession, how often he has gone to mass, how often he has said the rosary, how often he has said the *Our Father,* how many "Hail Marys" he has said, he checks whether he has received the last sacrament. And he runs through the list of the good deeds he has done.

A person's time in purgatory is determined by this analysis and whether he will ever to go heaven is too, because in this concept, eternal life depends on clean living and absolution of sins through the priesthood.

I realize that if I were talking with a Roman Catholic theologian, he might tell me that I wasn't quite accurate in describing the church's teaching.

But that's not the point. I am talking now as an ordinary, devout Roman Catholic. That's what I was, and I dare say such a description of the way of salvation is shared by many lay members of the church.

When you look at this way of salvation—this *analytic* way of salvation—you see that the ability of the human will is very important. As we have noticed, the Roman Catholic way of describing the fall of man into sin at the beginning of human history does not acknowledge the full degree of damage the fall caused. The Roman Church holds that the human intellect and the human will (and even human emotions) are still capable of some spiritual good. The church views Ephesians 2:1 as harsh but not absolute. Ephesians 2:1

describes Christians this way: "As for you, you were dead in your transgressions and sins, in which you used to live when you followed the ways of this world and the ruler of the kingdom of the air, the spirit who is now at work in those who are disobedient." Well, what does Ephesians 2:1 say? Dead is dead, isn't it? An English teacher would tell us that the adjective *dead* "does not admit of comparison."

The Roman Church does not recognize the total damage the fall has caused in natural man. The Bible says: "The man without the Spirit does not accept the things that come from the Spirit of God, for they are foolishness to him, and he cannot understand them, because they are spiritually discerned." (1 Corinthians 2:14)

When we examine what the Bible says about how we are saved, we see that its teaching is different from the teaching of the Roman Catholic Church that declares that human beings have the ability to make the first steps in God's direction. The Bible's message is that salvation is by grace alone, and it has to be this way because the natural man is dead as a door hinge when it comes to his ability to understand the way of salvation. You can yell and scream at a corpse all you want; it will not get up. You may change to a sweeter approach; it won't help in the least.

Now, once I saw that natural man was dead and that there was no such thing as free will in the sense that human beings after the fall had the ability to find their way back to God and do good works that would contribute to their salvation, I was led to the point where I had to believe in the biblical teaching of predestination. I had heard of it before and had just assumed it was false. I figured that it was the crazy idea of certain far right Protestants.

For me the word *predestination* (when I thought of it a time or two) was a synonym for *fatalism*. I assumed that Christians who believed in it had tumbled over the edge and were beyond hope of rescue.

As I studied the Bible, however, I discovered that what was clogging my brain was entirely different from the Bible's teaching regarding predestination.

In the Bible, predestination is a part of the great "grace alone" way of salvation. If salvation is not of man ("not of works so that no one can boast") it is and forever will be a human impossibility.

It is impossible for me to run the Boston Marathon. Look at me and you will see that I have legs, am fairly well built and presumably have a fairly good heart and pair of lungs somewhere in my chest, but I cannot run that marathon. Don't even ask me to train for it. And when it comes to salvation, I am dead by nature. I cannot take the first step.

What this means is that the only people who will ever be saved are those who are given true, saving faith by God. When we say that we are saved by grace, this means simply that God saves us. And when Ephesians 2 underscores this way of salvation by emphasizing *not of works*, it is telling us that we cannot save ourselves.

The Bible is actually very clear about this. In Ephesians 2 where it describes people who are under the influence "of the ruler of the kingdom of the air, the spirit who is now at work in those who are disobedient" as dead it goes on and describes the way God came into the lives of these dead people and gave them life. It says: "But because of his great love for us, God, who is rich in mercy, made us alive with Christ even when we were dead in transgressions—it is by grace you have been saved." Now here, you see, is a statement that lifts the whole matter of salvation out of the realm of human action and declares that salvation is from God alone. We cannot save ourselves any more than we can evolve ourselves into tigers. God makes the first move in salvation and he is part of every step that follows.

Now then, the word *predestination* actually refers to this fact: God makes the first move in salvation and he is part of every step that follows. It has to be this way because we are spiritually dead. The first chapter of Ephesians makes the connection between God's great work of salvation and predestination.

If you have never read these words before, hold your breath and remember that this is the Bible, inspired by the Holy Spirit. Here it is from Ephesians 1:3-8: "Praise be to the God and Father of our Lord Jesus Christ, who has blessed us in the heavenly realms with every spiritual blessing in Christ. For he chose us in him before the creation of the world to be holy and blameless in his sight. In love he predestined us to be adopted as his sons through Jesus Christ, in accordance with his pleasure and will—to the praise of his glorious grace, which he has freely given us in the One he loves. In him we have redemption through his blood, the forgiveness of sins, in accordance with the riches of God's grace that he lavished on us with all wisdom and understanding."

The devil has succeeded in convincing lots of people that *predestination* is just another word for fatalism. Satan has confused many people into thinking that predestination makes God a tyrant of some kind. But did you notice that predestination is about love and mercy? Look at this once again: "But because of his great love for us, God, who is rich in mercy, made us alive with Christ even when we were dead in transgressions—it is by grace you have been saved." (Ephesians 2:4,5) Predestination is the loving, merciful act of God who gives life to people who are dead. Reviving dead people is an act of God's "great love for us."

The predestination described in the Bible is by no means the fatalism that many people have made it. It is not some kind of divine lottery or some kind of arbitrary blue print crafted in heaven's courts that imposes a rigid, unyielding program on history. God's predestination is attached to a flesh and blood person who came and lived among us—the Lord Jesus Christ, who is the Second Person of the Divine Trinity.

I found out that the word *predestination* is part of a family of words that all refer to the same thing: *election* and *choice* are part of that family, too. And, if you look back at what we just noted in Ephesians 1 everything about these three words is related to the good things—the grace—believers have in Christ Jesus. We learn that what these words refer to is part of what Ephesians 1 calls God the Father's blessing in "the heavenly realms with every spiritual blessing in Christ" for those who are saved. Ephesians 1 emphasizes the fact that predestination has everything to do with blessing. Of course! After all, predestination is the source of life for people who would otherwise be dead!

Ephesians 1 also tells us that people who are so chosen are chosen to be a certain kind of people: "For he chose us in [Christ]...to be holy and blameless in [God's] sight." Those who are saved by God's good grace are not then free to live as they please, but they are people who are transformed so that they begin to look something like Christ.

And then, in Ephesians 1, the actual word *predestination* is used in connection with one of the tenderest ideas in the Bible. Notice this: "In love he predestined us to be adopted as his sons through Jesus Christ...." Now that's as good as it gets. I discovered that God the Father predestined me to be adopted as his son through Jesus Christ.

I admit these ideas leave me crushed. I will admit that when I consider the fact that salvation is God's work and not mine—he chose me before the creation of the world in Christ, he invaded my heart with his grace, and he will surely bring me to glory—when I consider this, I have all kinds of questions. They well up from inside me and knock on the doors of my brain. I think to myself: "Surely this can't be. Surely, I have something to do with my salvation." And sometimes, I wonder if God is being fair and then I remember that he was not in the least obligated to save me— he did it in love.

Most thinking people have these kinds of questions, and I believe that this is the reason Roman Catholicism is the biggest church within Christianity. Roman Catholicism tells people that they do have something to do with their salvation and that predestination simply means that God had perfect foreknowledge so that he knew who was going to decide to turn to him and be saved.

The reason I had finally to surrender and admit that the Bible's view of predestination makes God and God alone the source and the assurance of our salvation is that the Bible speaks of salvation in this way. The first two chapters of Ephesians, which we just looked at, surely make the sovereign God the source and assurance of salvation. Paul wrote this, as you know—he is my friend who visited my ancestors many years ago. But predestination is not found only in Paul's writings.

In John 10, Jesus himself describes himself as the Good Shepherd who knows his people, just as the Father knows him. We read in John 10:14-15: "I am the good shepherd; I know my sheep and my sheep know me—just as the Father knows me and I know the Father—and I lay down my life for the sheep." Jesus speaks here of his coming death and discloses that he died for a specific group of people whom he knew. He makes perfectly clear that when he died, he did not then have to wait to see if certain people would be sufficiently impressed to honor him with their faith. By no means. He died for *his people*. We might say that he died for "the elect," those who had been predestined for salvation.

In this same chapter, Jesus makes this same predestination the foundation of the certainty of salvation believers may have. If I have saving faith today, I know right from the get-go that I didn't create this faith myself: God gave it to me through his Holy Spirit. And if that is true, I know that God will not let me fall away. This is what Jesus says further in John 10:27-30—"My sheep listen to my voice; I know them, and they follow me. I give them eternal life, and they shall never perish; no one can snatch them out of my hand. My Father, who has given them to me, is greater than all; no one can snatch them out of my Father's hand. I and the Father are one." Now I am sure of my salvation. I never had that assurance in the Roman Church. But, you see, if salvation, is from God from beginning to end we can be sure that he cannot, he will not, save a person one year and toss him away a year later.

So, getting back to my friend the Apostle, it's no wonder that he talked about salvation the way he did. He also was enthusiastic about the way God carries our salvation all the way through to completion. He wrote to the Philippians that he was "confident of this, that he who began a good work in you will carry it on to completion until the day of Christ Jesus. (Philippians 1:6)

One main reason I assumed that the idea of predestination couldn't possibly be true was that I didn't really know anything about the Bible. Sad to say, the Roman Catholic Church gives its members the impression that they really don't have a high obligation to read the Bible because, after all, the lay people are not able to interpret it anyway—only the teaching church does that.

So, I never really knew the Bible. But once you get into the Bible and it throws its wonderful truth around within your heart, you can't miss the truth of predestination. Here are some of the sentences of the Bible that have made clear to me that salvation is of God and not of man. How do they strike you?

2 Timothy 1:9 – [God] has saved us and called us to a holy life—not because of anything we have done but because of his own purpose and grace. This grace was given us in Christ Jesus before the beginning of time.

Acts 13:48 – When the Gentiles heard this, they were glad and honored the word of the Lord; and all who were appointed for eternal life believed.

John 17:1-2 – "Father, the time has come. Glorify your Son, that your Son may glorify you. For you granted him authority over all people that he might give eternal life to all those you have given him.

John 17:9 – I pray for them. I am not praying for the world, but for those you have given me, for they are yours.

I discovered this in the Bible, once I started to read it and pray over it and attend a church where the Bible was the center of the church's life. As I heard the message preached, I was overwhelmed by the conviction: salvation is by grace alone, not of works, lest anyone boast.

Salvation—the Fruit of Predestination

It was humbling for me to learn from the Bible that my salvation was not the result of my decision or my careful attention to do what the Roman Catholic Church required me to do. And when I say it was humbling, I am not referring to the fairly fleeting feeling that we sometimes have when we do something dumb, like drive the wrong way down a one-way street. Once it begins to sink in that by nature you don't even have the ability to make the first decision to follow Christ and you are completely incapable of doing anything that will contribute to your salvation, you feel a humility that is deep and abiding. Gradually you find yourself thinking about God differently than you did before and thinking differently about yourself as well.

With regard to God, you begin to realize that being saved has nothing whatever to do with making some kind of a deal with God. I used to think that. I figured that if I did what was required of me, I would not have to worry too much about what would happen to me after my death; I would likely make it into heaven pretty quickly, even if I didn't get there right away. I viewed being saved as striking a good bargain with God. If I did my part, he would do his part. When I began to see that my salvation depended solely on God's mercy, I realized how confused I had been. There is no salvation deal in which sinners do their part and God does his. Salvation is from God and from God alone. And once I began to feel the humility that comes from seeing this, I felt a deep thankfulness to the Lord for what he had done for me. I found myself trying to please God out of a sense of deep gratitude.

With regard to myself, the humility that swept over my life made me experience a new peace and assurance. Because the way of salvation that I had been used to thinking about, required that I make sure that I do what had to be done, somewhere in the back of my brain there was always the question: "Have I done enough? What will happen if I come up short on God's balance sheet?" What would happen if I were nearly home free and I would commit a terribly serious sin and get run over by a Mack truck before I had a chance to go to confession? Or worse yet, what would happen if I would actually lose my faith? I realized that I could never be fully sure of my salvation while I was in this world.

But when I began to see that God was the source of my salvation, I realized that I was safe in his care. I knew that my trust in Christ's finished work for my salvation was God's new creation within me.

I realized that the faith I had was not the result of Joe Serge's personality traits, but it was the result of God's grace. Once these kinds of ideas penetrated my heart, I felt peace and security. If salvation is of God alone, I really don't have to worry about my ultimate destiny. The God who chose me in Christ and gave me my faith will one day welcome me into eternal glory for Jesus' sake. I have a glorious future, a very glorious future.

Well, this is very nice, and you can probably understand that trusting in God this way gave me a great deal of peace and joy. But there is a nagging question that bothered me as I began to make the switch from a devout Roman Catholic person to a person who believes that salvation is from God from first to last. There was a problem that bugged me, just as it does a lot of people. What does the biblical teaching regarding predestination do to the idea of free will? Roman Catholic teaching tells us that there is such a thing as free will, and we can use ours to make our first moves in God's direction and we can use it to do the good works that God wants to see in our lives.

Personally, I believe that the Roman teaching regarding free will is a major reason why this denomination appeals to so many. Because it teaches that salvation is in our power because salvation is the fruit of our decision it appeals to the way we are by nature. It's not very nice to discover that by nature you are unable to turn to the Lord. As the Apostle Paul puts it: "The man without the Spirit does not accept the things that come from the Spirit of God, for they are foolishness to him, and he cannot understand them, because they are spiritually discerned." (1 Corinthians 2:14) Without the Spirit of God, we are dead, and we cannot respond to the gospel call to repentance and faith. Talk about ideas that smash self-esteem, these ideas surely do.

The Bible also tells us that we cannot do anything that might possibly please God either unless we have the Spirit of Christ. The Bible also says: "The mind of the sinful man is death, but the mind controlled by the Spirit is life and peace; the sinful mind is hostile to God. It does not submit to God's law, nor can it do so. Those controlled by the sinful nature cannot please God." (Romans 8:6-8)

That is a devastating statement. Those controlled by the sinful nature—that's everyone who does not have the Spirit of God—cannot please God. Now, how does that make you feel?

When we look at the biblical teaching that people cannot make the first move toward God and they cannot do anything to please God by themselves, the natural human assumption that we have free will collapses. Oh, of course, we have a great deal of freedom with regard to relatively trivial matters. For example, we can decide to buy Nike running shoes instead of Adidas. We can decide to have dessert or skip it. We may even feel that we have freedom to choose to marry a certain person and not another one. True enough. But we are not talking about this kind of decision making; we are talking about whether or not we can decide to believe in the

God of the Bible and whether or not we can decide to live so that God is pleased with us.

The Bible crushes our confidence that we have free will. But as it does that it reveals something much more valuable than the imaginary free will that we thought we had. Though the Bible denies the existence of free will it reveals the reality of *freed* will. Because the issue whether or not we have free will is so important in understanding biblical religion, I want to talk briefly about freed will as this is described in Romans 6.

Romans 6 deals with a very natural conclusion that people made when they learned that salvation was not of works, but was by grace alone. If it is true that we cannot save ourselves with our own works, then some concluded that they could sin as much as they wanted to. As they put it: "Why don't we just go on sinning so that grace will increase?" Logical, yes, but false as the devil's smile.

The Apostle Paul reacted to this line of reasoning with vehemence. If I may paraphrase his response in the vernacular, he virtually said to people who thought this way: "Are you nuts?" To Paul the very idea that saved people could go on and live like moral idiots was preposterous. And it was preposterous because, when a person is saved by grace, that person is transformed. When people are saved by grace and their sins are washed away through the blood of Christ, signified by baptism, it is as if they have been buried with Christ in his death and raised to a new life.

Romans 6:4 says: "We were therefore buried with him through baptism into death in order that, just as Christ was raised from the dead through the glory of the Father, we too may live a new life." What this means according to Romans 6 is that a person who has been saved in this way is now dead to sin, but he is "alive to God in Christ Jesus." Therefore, such a person cannot, may not, consider living a life of sin. The salvation that is by grace and not of works creates a new life that is full of works that reflect the reality of salvation. A person who says he is saved, but lives like the devil wants him to live is not saved, even though he thinks he is.

What happens when a person is saved by God's grace is that the will of that person, which had been in bondage to sin before—it was not a free will—is freed from this bondage. Oh, it continues to be in bondage, but when a person is saved, his will is in bondage to righteousness. Romans 6:18 says to such a person: "You have been set free from sin and have become slaves to righteousness."

The human will is always a slave. It always is. Actually, we all know that. There is no such thing as free will. The great anti-Christian thought systems that define our modern age emphasize that human beings are driven by forces outside their control.

Darwinism declares that human beings are the product of chance evolutionary forces. Freudianism declares that human beings are the product of sexual drives. Marxism declares that human beings are driven by economic forces. These great worldviews, false as they are, are joined today by natural scientific theories that tell us that we have been programmed from conception to be what we are. Psychologists put human beings in a box they cannot escape.

When you start thinking about free will, you discover that religious leaders have emphasized it the most. In the history of Christian thought it was the third century theologian Pelagius who rejected the Bible's teaching of the bondage of the human will and suggested that human beings were not terribly affected by the fall of man into sin. He said they retained the freedom to turn to God and do good things. This thinking became the foundation of the popular religion that we associate with Roman Catholicism. Though some Roman Catholic theologians today realize that free will does not really exist, ordinary Roman Catholics, as I was when I was growing up and later as an adult, are given the impression that their salivation depends on their personal free will.

It does not. It does not because there is no such thing as free will. There is no such thing as free will that is able to choose for God and for good works. But, praise God, there is such a thing as *freed* will. And when I left the Roman Church and received the truth of the Bible, I discovered the wonder of freed will. That most surely exists, but that, too, like everything else in salvation, is a gift of God.

Predestination, the free, sovereign choice of the Father of my Lord Jesus Christ, is the fountain from which everything about salvation flows. It is God's Spirit that works in our hearts and causes us to turn from our evil ways and flee to Christ. This great biblical truth was re-discovered at the time of the Protestant Reformation.

The Reformer John Calvin wrote, "God, therefore, begins the good work by exciting in our hearts a desire, a love, and a study of righteousness." Calvin wrote about the way God acts on the dead will of sinful human beings; he says: "I say the will is abolished, but not in so far as it is [a] will, for in conversion everything essential to our original nature remains: I also say, that it is created anew, not because the will then begins to exist, but because it is turned from evil to good."

R.C. Sproul, a contemporary teacher of salvation through grace alone, reflects what we saw the Apostle Paul write in Romans 6. In his book *Willing to Believe*, Sproul writes: "It is precisely this work of God that liberates the sinner from slavery. It is a strange thing to deem the liberation of an enslaved will as a violation of freedom. It is God's work of freeing, not violating, that is in view."

Now, I want to admit that the biblical teaching that roots human salvation in God's free and sovereign choice raises some questions and I wrestled with them. A book like this is not the place to deal with these questions in depth. But I was a newspaperman for many years, and a columnist, and I want to note these questions as items of full disclosure. I want you to know that these bothered me.

Problem 1 – The fact that the salvation of any person flows from God's sovereign choice raises the question of God's justice. If God elected some to salvation and not others, wasn't he being unjust and unfair?

Let me just say that there are several passages in the Bible that address this issue. The main passage for me is found in Romans 9:14-15 where the Bible says: "Is God unjust? Not at all! For he says to Moses, "I will have mercy on whom I have mercy and I will have compassion on whom I have compassion." These words, which are a quotation from the Old Testament, imply that we must remember that because the fall of man into sin occurred, God had the right to send every human being to hell. All human beings are disobedient and liable to receive eternal punishment. That God elected to save any at all is because of his mercy. That he passed others by is his divine prerogative.

In this same chapter, the Apostle Paul reminds us of the difference between our dealing with proper questions and improper questions. In Romans 9:19-21 we read: "One of you will say to me: 'Then why does God still blame us? For who resists his will?' But who are you, O man, to talk back to God? Shall what is formed say to him who formed it, 'Why did you make me like this?' Does not the potter have the right to make out of the same lump of clay some pottery for noble purposes and some for common use?"

I do not want to suggest that material like this in the Bible leaves me fully satisfied. But I must remember the absolute right of God to do what he determines is just. I am a human being with limited thoughts and insights, so I must simply say: the potter has the right to make the clay anyway he so desires. There is a great mystery here, something that causes us to put our hands over our mouths and become silent. We who are limited are humbled before the wonder of God's great being.

Problem 2 – If salvation is rooted in divine predestination, doesn't this make human decision and action impossible and meaningless? The logical answer would be: yes it does. But logic is not the ultimate issue in true religion. Anyone whose thought has been formed by a deep and continual reading of the Bible knows that the Bible continually emphasizes the significance of human action and decision

Remember, we saw that the great thought systems that have formed modernity all declare that human beings are controlled by some force or another—natural selection, sexual drives, economic laws. Anyone who thinks deeply about human freedom will discover that it does not really exist; it is more apparent than real. A good example of that is the so-called *pro-choice* movement that Satan uses to assure the death of millions of pre-born babies. This dreadful movement is built on the idea of free choice, but when you question women who abort their children, they will usually tell you that as much as they hate abortion, they were forced to destroy their child. Some force, real or imagined, made them feel compelled. When we read the Bible, we learn that when a person is saved by Christ's grace, then, for the first time, that person is free to make proper decisions.

The Bible makes human choice extremely important in the matter of salvation. When a Philippian prison warden asked the Apostle Paul what he should do to be saved, the apostle made no reference whatsoever to predestination. If you read Acts 16:30-31, you learn that the apostle simply told him, "Believe in the Lord Jesus, and you will be saved—you and your household." The Bible is full of incidents in which people are told to believe in Christ. In fact, they are told to believe because when the good news of salvation is presented, God energizes what was before a dead human will, so that many who hear the gospel become able to respond with saving faith.

Problem 3 – This problem is closely related to the previous problem. Problem three is the question of the church's mission. If salvation depends on the predestination of God, why should the church do any mission work?

What has helped me greatly is the fact that the three Bible chapters that deal most directly with the matter of predestination—election—Romans 9,10,11 also contain one of the most powerful calls to mission found anywhere in the Scriptures.

Romans 10 starts with the Apostle Paul bemoaning the fact that so many of his fellow Jews had rejected Christ and would, therefore, perish. But right here, where he expresses dismay that many Jews rejected Christ, Paul describes how people are saved exclusively in terms of their personal reaction to Christ. In Romans 10:9-10 we read: "If you confess with your mouth, 'Jesus is Lord, and believe in your heart that God raised him from the dead, you will be saved. For it is with your heart that you believe and are justified, and it is with your mouth that you confess and are saved." He also says, in the same context, "Anyone who trusts in [Christ] will never be put to shame." And he says, again in the same chapter: "Everyone who calls on the name of the Lord, will be saved." (Romans 10:11,13)

You see, even though our small minds cannot understand how the Bible can be unmistakable in its declaration that salvation is rooted in the work of God that we call predestination while it stresses the responsibility of those who hear the gospel to believe the gospel, that's really okay.

When it comes to salvation, there are many things that sinners like us will never understand. I don't think we will understand them in glory. All we can do when we see the great mercy of God expressed in predestination in Christ is marvel. That is exactly how the great chapters on predestination and election conclude in the Bible.

Listen to these exalted words:

"Oh, the depths of the riches of the wisdom and knowledge of God! How unreachable his judgments and his paths beyond tracing out! "Who has known the mind of the Lord? Or who has been his counselor? Who has ever given to God that God should repay him?" For from him and through him and to him are all things. To him be the glory forever! Amen." – Romans 11:33-36

Or to put it in the words of an anonymous hymn writer, all that anyone who reads the Bible carefully and believes it is the written Word of God can say, is this:

> *I sought the Lord, and afterward I knew*
> *He moved my soul to seek him, seeking me*
> *It was not I that found, O Savior, true;*
> *No I was found, was found of thee.*

VII

JESUS PAID IT ALL

If you have been paying attention to the last several pages,
you may well be thinking that it's perfectly okay with you that
I have had problems with the Roman Catholic Church and
have consequently left it. Lots of people have done that,
many of them for fairly trivial reasons. But religion is every
person's own business. Why try to get other people to see
that there is something basically wrong with being a Roman
Catholic? Why should I present material that might possibly
convince others to follow the path that has led me to peace
and joy?

I recognize that the prevalent view regarding religion is
that it is a personal matter and that precisely what a person
believes doesn't make any difference. After all, many people
assume that one religion is as good as another; if you want to
be a Buddhist, no problem. And if you are a Christian and
one branch of the Christian faith appeals to you more than
another, feel free to do whatever makes you comfortable.
And, of course, so far as Roman Catholicism is concerned,
uncounted numbers of people just get tired of it, or they may
be scandalized by the conduct of certain priests or some such
thing, and they just forget their former religion altogether. In
any case, it's no big deal, one way or the other.

There are basically two reasons why I feel compelled to
get this message out. The most important is that true, biblical
religion brings honor to God. That is very important. No

one of us should dishonor God. If we do that, we put our lives and our futures in the gravest of danger. God does not overlook dishonor of his being and of his name. You may have heard that the third commandment that tells us we are not to use God's name improperly also tells us, "the Lord will not hold any one guiltless who misuses his name." (Exodus 20:7) We may not dishonor God, and therefore it is important that we read the Bible carefully in order to determine what religion is true and what is false. God is pleased when people like us worship him properly; divine wrath and jealousy are his reaction when we do not.

The other reason I want to share what I have found to be true with others follows from what I have just said about bringing proper honor to God. If we dishonor God and corrupt the pure gospel that we find in the Bible, we place ourselves in spiritual danger. I do not want to say that everyone who follows the Roman Catholic faith will be condemned eternally, but, many will be; therefore I feel compelled to share what I have found. My prayer is that many will see the central teaching of the Bible and joyfully embrace it.

There is a central, fundamental flaw in Roman Catholicism that contradicts biblical religion. If you are a person of good conscience and you want to honor the true God, you should know about this flaw. If you are a person who longs for assurance of salvation, you should know about this flaw because this flaw is keeping you from the joy and peace you could have if you were trusting Christ only for your salvation. We must all examine our hearts and minds to make sure that we are properly honoring God for what he has done to save sinners like us.

Many people nowadays agree that religion is important but they don't think that precisely what religion you follow makes any difference. They are wrong. There are thousands of different religions (actually millions depending on how you count), but only one of them is true. And you owe it to God and to yourself to know that religion. If you miss it for whatever reason your eternal destiny is bleak.

Yes, there are countless religions and variations on the religion theme in the world, but when you examine all of them in the light of the Bible, there are actually only two religions—only two. And what are they?

There are many religions that tell us that salvation depends on human works—that's one kind of religion. The one true religion, described in the Bible tells us that salvation does not depend on human works. It is, as I have been stressing, based on God's mercy at every point. It is rooted in God's action, not man's action. True religion is "Amazing Grace" religion. These are the two classifications: "Works Religion" and "Amazing Grace" religion.

This is a good classification to use when you examine the great religions of the world. When you study them, you will find that all of the non-Christian religions emphasize human action if a person is to be saved. Even Buddhism does, though it is virtually an atheistic religion because it does not emphasize deity as such—but Buddhism describes the possibility of movement to ever higher forms of consciousness that depends on how people conduct themselves in this life. And nowadays we all know that Islam offers Paradise to its followers as a reward for what they do in this life—going on *jihad* will guarantee an exciting, even erotic, experience in Paradise. Perhaps this is why suicide bombers do what they do.

And within Christianity itself there are also groups that teach, or give the impression, that salvation depends on how faithfully people live in this world. Roman Catholicism has carefully developed the idea that salvation depends on our works. When I was a boy growing up I figured that if my sins were going to be forgiven, I had to go to confession and be absolved by a priest who would give me a nominal penance such as reciting a few Hail Marys, the Our Father and a Glory Be.

Sometimes I would go to confession and tell the priest what was on my conscience and then, after I had left, I would remember something I had forgotten to tell him and I would be worried about my salvation.

If you are a Roman Catholic you know the church's teaching about purgatory. In Roman Catholic teaching, saved people go to purgatory, but they go there because, even though they are saved, they are not sufficiently pure to be allowed into heaven. In purgatory they are purified further, and once they have been brought up to the accepted standard of purity, they may enter heaven. In other words, the salvation of the faithful depends on whether or not they are good enough to enter heaven. The Bible tells us that if we believe in Jesus Christ, his righteousness becomes our righteousness and we go directly to heaven when we die.

The church teaches that purgatory is a place where believers go to be purified from the stain their many sins have made upon their person. If they have been especially rebellious sinners in this life, they may have to spend a long time there; if they have been exceptionally holy, they won't have to spend very long. But purgatory is there because most people cannot reach a state of holiness sufficient to allow them to enter heaven directly. It's interesting that nowadays the church doesn't talk about purgatory very much, but it is there, in its latest catechism.

Purgatory is not taught in the Bible. Oh, I know that there are a couple of texts that you can use to support it if you are willing to stretch them. If you are looking for texts to support the idea that after this life believers spend time in purgatory so that they can be purified further, there are apocryphal writings relating to the Maccabees that you can use, but the Apocrypha is not part of the accepted canon of the Bible.

The basic support for purgatory comes from the notion that saved people cannot actually go to heaven unless their souls are brought up to standard by a post-death purification process. That's because other than martyrs and other extremely pious people no one can do enough good to offset the impact of the evil they've done in this world, and need to spend some time in that place. The purgatory idea is a good one if our entrance into heaven depends on what we are. On the other hand, if Christ paid for the sins of his people once and for all at the cross of Calvary and met every requirement for their entrance into heaven, purgatory is a very bad idea.

Why is purgatory bad?

It's bad because it undercuts the message of the cross. It undercuts the central biblical teaching that our entrance into heaven depends on Jesus alone—that salvation depends on the work of just one man, and that man is Jesus. And that man, according to the Bible, is also God. So we must say that salvation depends only on the work of God. As we have noted several times, we cannot pay for our sins because we don't have the currency that can pay for them and we cannot do anything to make us pure enough to go to heaven. If Christ has not taken care of all this, we are hopelessly lost.

What do we have to offer in payment for our sins? Every single act, every single gift, every single anthem of praise, every single work we put forward in payment for our sin is itself contaminated by our sin. We are in the ultimate Catch-22 situation: our sins must be paid for but every time we try to pay for them ourselves we increase our sin. We increase our sin because the greatest sin is to think for the briefest of moments that there is anything we can do to save ourselves. We can do nothing to save ourselves. And if we think that we can have experiences in this life or in a purgatory to come that will make us so pure that we can enter heaven and stand next to the holy angels, we are seriously mistaken.

Why am I going to the trouble of putting this book in your hands? Let's just say, for purposes of discussion, that yes, there are some things wrong with the Roman Catholic

Church, but what's so terrible about that? There are things wrong with all religion. Do we have to find the perfect religion to be saved? After all, if salvation is by grace alone, we shouldn't even worry about whether the religion we follow is exactly right.

Well, that would be true except that what is wrong with Roman Catholicism and with all religion that contradicts the Bible is that the error is fatal. There are errors and there are errors; some will not cause death but others will. Just like with our diets: none of us eats a perfect diet, some people eat way too many mammoth Whopper cheeseburgers for example. Thankfully, our bodies are usually forgiving. But try eating arsenic. You won't last long. So, too, when it comes to religion nobody has it hundred percent right. True. But when a religion consistently, century after century presents ideas that tear the heart out of the religion of the Bible, there are bound to be many casualties. A system of teaching that tells us that Jesus didn't do enough to assure us that when we close our eyes in death we will immediately open them in glory, denies the essence of biblical religion.

Now then, what, or who, is the heart of Christianity? Jesus is. That's right, but it's not the full story. The heart of the Christian faith is the crucifixion of Jesus Christ of Nazareth. The cross is the heart of the Bible, the cross is the heart of Christianity, and the same cross is at the very heart of God himself.

Christianity is not merely an inspirational religion that gives those who follow it warm, fuzzy feelings about themselves and about God. It is not merely an attractive religion because it provides a feast for our senses. Christianity is the religion that tells us how God has accomplished the salvation of believers. The Bible is the record of Almighty God's reaction to the sin of humankind. The sin of humankind goes all the way back to the very first sin in Paradise and it includes every sin that has ever been committed and ever will be. Obviously, I do not know the people who read this book, but I can say this with certainty about every one of them: each one is a sinner whom God has every right to cast into hell because of his or her sin. This is true of me and it's true of you.

Every problem that bothers us pales in comparison with the fact that by nature we are on death row, eternal death row. Without the intervention of God, every one of us would experience eternal punishment. The Bible tells us how God himself intervened in this unspeakably horrible situation and did exactly what had to be done so that believers can escape this ghastly fate.

It was at the cross where the great work of salvation was finally accomplished. We have talked about the way the Bible reveals that the work of salvation had its origin in the Father's choosing his people "before the foundation of the earth." But that truth does not stand alone. The eternal decree of God required that on a certain day in history the actual Son of God, living in the reality of world history, would be attached to a cross outside Jerusalem where he would receive the punishment required by God's righteousness as payment for human sin. The cross is the absolute center of the Christian faith, it is the center of world history, and it is the center of all reality. The cross is the supreme manifestation of the nature of God and it shows us that God is a God of indescribable love. Because of this, any religion that compromises the full meaning of the cross is fundamentally dangerous.

A form of Christianity that wants to be known as authentic but that suggests in any way that Christ's sacrifice for sin was not enough, or not quite enough, to make it possible for believers to enter into glory is not authentic biblical religion. Religion that tells its followers that Christ did a great deal on the cross but that they now must do their part to supplement Christ's less than adequate sacrifice becomes guilty of being the opposite of what God intends true religion to be. We do not have a problem seeing this in the case of non-Christian religions, but it is much more difficult to see this in the various forms of Christianity that promote a *grace plus works* program of salvation.

In my journey from a works righteousness form of religion, I was guided by the strong leadership of my friend from Malta, the Apostle Paul, who as I noted at the beginning was once shipwrecked on the very island where my forebears lived. He was an inveterate traveler, and during the course of his wanderings, he established many churches. As all pastors and missionaries, there were many times when he tore out his hair in despair because of how people who had heard the true gospel from him later turned away. He became especially upset with the Christians in the province of Galatia. The New Testament book of Galatians contains his response to the way they first believed the gospel of grace, but later, under the influence of false teachers, they fell back into a teaching that declared that they had to supplement what Jesus had done on the cross with their own careful keeping of the law.

If you would read through Galatians, you would sense the apostle's outrage, and you would see how he felt compelled to condemn the false direction the Galatians were going. Paul begins the book by stressing that the gospel of salvation by faith alone, by grace alone, that what he had brought to these people was not something he had dreamed up. He writes: "I did not receive it from any man, nor was I taught it; rather, I received it by revelation from Jesus Christ." (1:12)

Now, I would like to quote a few more sentences from Galatians that contain the term *works of the law*. When I cite these, just remember that that phrase refers to trying to do something for your salvation by your own works. In the second chapter of this book, the Apostle Paul shows that we are either saved by God's grace alone, through faith in Jesus Christ, or we are saved by works, or, as he calls it, "by the works of the law." You can't have it both ways. And the reason you can't have it both ways becomes clear as he concludes what I am now going to quote. Notice this: *We who are Jews by birth and not Gentile sinners know that a man is not justified by observing the law, but by faith in Jesus Christ. So we, too, have put our faith in Christ Jesus that we may be justified by faith in Christ and not by observing the law, because by observing the law no one will be justified. (2:15-16)*

He then explains that through faith in Christ, believers are joined to Christ and his virtue becomes theirs. He describes this in very dramatic language; this is what he writes:

I have been crucified with Christ and I no longer live, but Christ lives in me. The life I now live in the body, I live by faith in the Son of God, who loved me, and gave himself for me. I do not set aside the grace of God, for if righteousness could be gained through the law, Christ died for nothing! (2:20-21)

I hope you see how the Bible puts the issue here. The Apostle sets up an either/or situation: either we are saved by the cross of Christ or we are not. We cannot say that we are saved by the cross *plus* what we ourselves do to please God, nor even plus some purification process that occurs after death that brings us up to heaven's standard. The Apostle points out that if you think that your salvation depends on Christ's work plus your work, then Christ died for nothing. To think that salvation has anything to do with works is actually a serious criticism of the way of salvation that God has provided. What we are actually saying when we say something like that is that Christ did a lot but he couldn't to the whole job. He needs our help.

I began to see that it's not that way at all. Christ did not need my help so that I could be saved. Jesus paid it all! The only thing I have to do is believe in Christ, that is all. There is nothing I can do to save myself. Salvation is of God and of God alone. In Ephesians 2:9, right after the Apostle describes the way we are saved by grace through faith and not of works, he adds, "so that no one can boast." You see, if we did the slightest thing to save ourselves, we could boast. When it comes to salvation we have nothing whatsoever to boast about.

For human beings to think that they can do something to save themselves is a terrible sin against Almighty God who has done everything necessary to save us: he has sent his only begotten Son, the Son of his eternal love, to a cross to die for our sins. It is a great error to thank him for saving us, while at the same time we believe that he couldn't finish achieving our salvation without our help.

This is a terrible deformation of the truth of the gospel. Oh, there are a lot of flaws in all of our religious lives, but this is the most damaging. A car will run with a lot of things wrong with it, but if you put water in the gas tank, that will be the end of it. So, too, there are various errors that can mar a religious position, but the error that suggests that our works contribute in some degree to our salvation destroy the Bible's central message, and religion that is built on this idea cannot be repaired.

VIII

PRIDE

As you can see, I have had a fascinating journey. When you move from a religious way that surrounded you with a carefully structured set of requirements for salvation to the biblical religion that reveals that salvation is by grace alone, you begin to wonder what it was that caused you to be so deeply involved in the religion of works in the first place. As I have thought about this I have concluded that my problem was pride.

There is such a thing as good pride, of course. The apostle Paul was proud of the people who had come to faith in Christ and had become an example to others. He wrote to one of the churches he had worked with, "Among God's churches we boast about your perseverance and faith in all the persecutions and trials you are enduring." (2 Thessalonians 1:4) Obviously, the apostle was proud of these people, and he let them know it.

But most pride is detrimental because it is self-centered and self-serving. There is no good that can be said for it. The Bible tells us that God opposes the proud. (James 4:6; 1 Peter 5:5) *Pride* and *sin* are virtually equivalent terms.

It was pride that led Satan to rebel against God. There is a poetic description of Satan's fall from morning star status to the pit of the hell in Isaiah 14:12-15. Isaiah was writing about Babylon, but Babylon's plunge from glory to crushing defeat is used to let us sense something of what happened in the original rebellion in the courts of heaven when Satan took his stand against God. "How you have fallen from heaven, O morning star, son of the dawn! You have been cast down to the earth, you who once laid low the nations! You said in your heart, 'I will ascend to heaven; I will raise my throne above the stars of God; I will sit enthroned on the mount of assembly, on the utmost heights of the sacred mountain. I will ascend above the tops of the clouds; I will make myself like the Most High.' But you are brought down to the grave, to the depths of the pit."

Since Satan is a master of pride, it is not surprising that he caused the Fall to occur by inciting pride in our first parents. We know that Adam and Eve lived amid perfection; their every need was met and, most important, they had direct contact with God himself. When Satan approached Eve, he stirred her pride and made her feel that God was not treating her fairly. As we say: "the rest is history," and a horribly sad history it is.

The origin of our misery is revealed in a brief statement: "Now the serpent was more crafty than any of the wild animals the Lord God had made. He said to the woman, 'Did God really say, "You must not eat from any tree in the garden?" (Genesis 3:1) Then, when the woman explained that they were not to eat of it on pain of death, Satan flatly contradicted God's statement. The serpent said: "You will not surely die."

As you know, Adam, the covenant head of the human race and the head of his marriage, was also overcome by the stirrings of pride, and together, our parents decided to disobey God. Satan had exalted himself above God and he determined to make sure that the first human being he met would try to do the same. He succeeded horribly well, and we all suffer because of his success.

Nowhere does pride operate with greater effectiveness than in the realm of religion. The history of mankind is the history of countless attempts to create forms of religion that make it unnecessary for us to humble ourselves before God and repent of our sins and receive our salvation on God's terms. Some of the most outrageous examples of man-made religion that engenders pride are found within the Bible itself. The Pharisees, a religious sect that arose after Judah's return from the Babylonian captivity and that flourished when Jesus was on earth, transformed the law of God into something they could use to rise to what they thought was high moral achievement. They were so damn proud that Jesus bluntly told them they were going to hell.

Matthew 23 is one of the most scathing chapters in the Bible. "You snakes! You brood of vipers! How will you escape being condemned to hell?" So Jesus spoke to them. He spoke this way because they tried to lift themselves above the common herd by their good works. But in this same chapter, Jesus points out that this is not the way of salvation—it's the way of condemnation. Pride smells like smoke; it wafts over our lives from hell's underworld. True religion is the opposite of the works righteousness the Pharisees sought to establish for themselves. In Matthew 23:13 Jesus describes saving religion this way: "Whoever exalts himself will be humbled, and whoever humbles himself will be exalted."

In the well-known Sermon on the Mount, Jesus warns that the way of Pharisaical works righteousness salvation is doomed to failure. He says: "I tell you that unless your righteousness surpasses that of the Pharisees and the teachers of the law, you will certainly not enter the kingdom of heaven." (Matthew 5:20)

I have come to love the way an old catechism describes the way of salvation by grace alone. The Heidelberg Catechism is one of the precious documents that have come down to us from the rich faith experience of those who were willing to die for their faith at the time of the Protestant Reformation. The Catechism is divided into 52 Lord's Days, and Lord's Day 23 raises this question: "How are you right with God?" Listen to this answer: "Even though my conscience accuses me of having grievously sinned against all God's commandments and of never having kept any of them, and even though I am still inclined toward all evil, nevertheless, without my deserving it at all, out of sheer grace, God grants and credits to me the perfect satisfaction, righteousness, and holiness of Christ, as if I had never sinned nor been a sinner, as if I had been as perfectly obedient as Christ was obedient for me."

This statement captures the good news of the Bible: we are saved by grace alone—by *sheer grace*. Now, if it is true that we are saved by grace, why is it that so many of us prefer a way of salvation that depends on what we do in addition to what God does? Why do we like a grace *plus* form of religion? Why? Well, if I look at myself and some of my close friends who are still Roman Catholics, I believe that we naturally prefer a form of religion that makes us part of the salvation team, along with Triune God, because of our pride. We don't really want to humble ourselves totally beneath the mighty hand of God so that he can exalt us. We want to have something to do with this exaltation—we really do want to be on the team with God.

I believe that Roman Catholicism is as successful as it is because it offers people like me a way of salvation that gives me a chance to participate in salvation myself. As we often say nowadays: "I can have ownership in the process." For me, the Roman Catholic way appealed to my pride. Many things about the Roman way made me feel important and very religious.

From my childhood, I believed in the power of medals, sacred relics, crucifixes, incense, rosary beads, votive candles, holy water, prayers for the dead and indulgences. All these were part of the sacred furniture of my life. Just thinking about them, reading about them, and occasionally actually having a chance to view one of the relics inspired me.

As you likely know, a relic can take the form of a small piece of bone from a saint's body, or it may be another part of a saint, long dead—it could be a strand of a saint's hair, or a bit of her clothing. Some relics are supposed to be a piece of wood or a nail from the Jesus' cross. The Basilica of St. Mary Major in Rome boasts a relic said to be a fragment from Jesus' birth crib. At St. Anthony's basilica in Padua, Italy, the tongue and jawbone of this Italian saint who died in 1231 lies within a glass case. In 1263, in Orvieto, Italy, witnesses claimed to see human blood drip from the Eucharist wafer and stain the linen altar cloth; the host and blood-stained linen are now encased in a special shine in Orvieto's cathedral, and the event became the origin of The Feast of Corpus Christi.

Today there is still great interest in relics such as these: in 2000 nearly 25 million holy year pilgrims visited Rome's relic-filled shrines.

And the church made the veneration and use of relics and all the rest seem reasonable to me, so long as I didn't examine the way the church was using the Bible. There are events in the Bible that suggest that physical contact with relics, or at least visiting their location, can help us. In 2 Kings 13:21, we read of a man who was raised to life as soon as his body touched the prophet Elisha's bones. Numbers 21:4-9 tells how God sent poisonous snakes among the people of Israel to punish them for their idolatry; he then instructed Moses to make a bronze snake and raise it on a pole so that those who looked at it could be healed. Matthew 9:20-22 tells of a woman who suffered from chronic bleeding for many years, who was healed when she touched the edge of Jesus' cloak. Acts 19:12 tells how people took handkerchiefs that had touched the Apostle Paul back to the sick and they were healed.

The Roman Church sees these and similar reports in the Bible as justification for its use of relics. Of course, relics are appealing to common people who do not really know the

Bible, but when you examine the Bible carefully, there is no record of any material thing or substance having miraculous powers. In fact, the snake on the pole described in Numbers 21 became a source of false religion for the Jews. The snake became a relic, and during the reign of Hezekiah, it was destroyed because of the people of Israel had been burning incense to it. In 2 Kings 18:1-4 we read how it was broken into pieces right along with all the other pagan relics that were corrupting the people.

The remarkable resurrection of the man thrown in Elisha's tomb is much like the great vision of dry bones that we find in Ezekiel 37. The dry bones came to life when the Holy Spirit blew across them. These events were dramatic prophecies that pointed forward to the day when apostate Israel would be renewed through the presence of the Holy Spirit.

There were certainly many miracles during Jesus' ministry and the apostolic time. They served a special role in demonstrating that a new era had entered world history. They accompanied the new, strange gospel message when it came into Asia Minor and similar places. We can also expect miracles these days when we confront unbelief in areas where there is no knowledge of Christianity whatsoever or deep hatred of the Christian faith. But this is something different from attributing miraculous power to a shred of cloth or a chip of wood or a drop of blood or a single hair.

It was not until I became more fully aware of the biblical message that I began to see that the system of religion that invited me to become involved in my own salvation by using medals that had been blessed and faithfully using the special relics Rome provided was opposed to the way of salvation that is by grace alone. I wanted to hold onto all this; it strengthened me in some perverse way. It made me feel that I was doing at least something to insure my eternal well-being. Gradually, I began to see the Roman way as something that had been largely fabricated by human beings in order to keep the faithful dependent on the church.

I thank God that through the centuries there has always been much in the Roman Catholic Church that has reflected the truth of God. There were flashes of light during the so-called "dark ages" that enabled people to see Jesus with clarity. But I thank God even more that he now gives to many of us the opportunity to turn directly to the Bible ourselves so that we can move beyond the Roman way into the bright light of the truth that sets us free. I now see that Christ is my Savior who has paid it all. My debt was paid fully at the cross and I need nothing more for my salvation. Nothing!

My pride that was built on the feeling that I had something to do with my own salvation has been crushed. In its place, I can say only: "Thank you, Jesus!"

IX

GRACE FOR NOW AND FOREVER

Is there any way that we can know for sure that we are saved?
Many people figure that they will surely be saved because of
their pedigree; for them it's almost like having the proper
papers for a pure bred dog. They claim that their parents and
their grandparents were Christians so they must be Christians,
too. I guess you would say they have "designer genes." Well,
salvation has nothing to do with our genes.

When you examine your own thoughts about your
salvation, you may have to admit that you tend to think that
it has something to do with family background. And yet, if I
asked you: are you sure that you are saved, you would
probably say that you cannot be perfectly sure. You
probably feel that it would be presumptuous for you to say
that you are sure. You just have to wait and see what
happens when you die and you "meet St. Peter at the gate of
heaven," as is often said.

In my Roman Catholic days, I always sought God's
pardon at the confessional booth, and I would pray that I
would not die before I had confessed every serious sin to a
priest. Everything depended on the absolution the priest
would give me. Even so, I knew I was not perfect, and I
expected that after I died, I would spend a certain amount of
time in purgatory where my final purification would take
place. I hoped that time would be short.

But always there was the nagging doubt that I might not make it into heaven at all because I might die before confessing a serious sin. After all, you just never know what you might do before you die. One thing was clear to me: I needed the church if I was going to be saved.

The church promised me a way of salvation through a grace that is different from the grace of salvation I now possess. When you read the latest Roman Catholic catechism, grace is described in a number of ways. But for the ordinary, garden-variety follower of the Roman Church, grace is connected with the sacraments. In fact, the picture I had in my mind was a picture of grace as a virtual substance of some kind that was dispensed by the sacraments. It is almost as if the sacraments were like faucets through which grace flowed into believers' lives. And the church turned the faucets on and off—that's what I thought.

Roman doctrine says a person is safe so long as he has received sufficient sacramental grace for salvation. The dispensing of grace begins with baptism; this sacrament neutralizes the power of original sin. This is followed by the grace of confirmation and the grace of the absolution that the priest gives sinners when they make their confession. If a person is in a proper state of grace, he may attend mass and receive Holy Communion, which is the primary dispenser of grace in the Roman Church. By partaking of the sacred elements that the church presents as the actual, physical body and blood of Christ, a person is placed in a state of grace that provides a high degree of safety. And I prayed that, before drawing my last breath, I would receive the final sacrament, the Anointing of the Sick, just before death.

I believed that priests receive their own sacrament, and married people receive the sacrament of marriage. The church is the custodian of seven sacraments that together provide the faithful with the grace they need in order to be saved. However, if anything happens to separate a person from this ecclesiastical provision of grace, that person is in great trouble. If he is excommunicated from the church, the person is anathema. And anathema means *cursed;* it means *damned.* This is all very scary. Even if a person manages to escape hell, there's a good chance that he will spend a long time being purified in purgatory, and that spells torment.

As I read the Bible, I discovered that grace was not something like a substance that the church dispenses. Many of the letters that the Apostle Paul writes to the churches begin with a holy greeting that says, "Grace and peace to you from God our Father and the Lord Jesus Christ." (1 Corinthians 1:3)

The grace of which he speaks is the unearned favor of God that comes into the lives of those who trust in Christ for their salvation. When I surrendered to Jesus and asked him to take over my life as my personal Savior, I was instantly pardoned, sealed and saved for eternal life. My salvation is now secure. Nothing can take it away. Nothing. And I will spend no time in purgatory because there is no purgatory.

I do not claim that my surrender to Christ was caused by some personal ability or quality. I know that my very turning away from my own works to the finished work of Christ was caused by the Holy Spirit within me. I take no credit for my faith. I keep going back to what Ephesians 2:8-9 says: "For it is by grace you have been saved, through faith—and this not of yourselves, it is the gift of God—not by works, so that no one can boast." Salvation is God's work through and through.

I have been saved by grace alone; God gave me my faith and God graciously applied the perfect righteousness of Christ to my poor life. I have peace. I am confident that the day I die, I will enter the presence of God. My sins are many, and I confess them to my Savior every day; they will not be counted against me when I stand before the judge of all the earth, Jesus Christ. The person who would have every reason to condemn me is the very person who died for me, rose again and who now intercedes daily on my behalf. (Romans 8:33-34)

But now there's a problem. If what we do has nothing to do with whether or not we are saved, what about the way we live each day? If we are saved by grace alone, apart from works, what happens when you get up in the morning and have sixteen hours to fill? May you live as you please? There have been some who have responded to the way of salvation I have just described by saying that this gives them license to live like the devil. After all, if they are saved by grace apart from their works, they can do whatever they want.

There is nothing new under the sun, and this line of thought is as old as the hills. The Apostle Paul refers to it in Romans 6:1 when asks: "Shall we go on sinning so that grace may increase?" That might seem logical, but it contradicts the good news of salvation found in the Bible. The Bible tells us that those who have been saved through the finished work of Christ are enabled, through Christ's Holy Spirit in their lives, to live transformed lives.

I like to think of grace as being God's way of saving us for eternity and also God's way of transforming our lives during our earthly journey. Believers are saved by grace alone because nothing they do can contribute to their salvation. They must say: "Nothing in my hands I bring, simply to thy cross I cling." And once that happens, the grace of God enters their lives and transforms them. God's saving grace affects everything they do. Grace is not only there to assure us that our forever will be spent in glory, but grace also enables us to begin to live God glorifying lives in this world. The Roman Catholic Church is correct when it emphasizes the necessity of fighting sin and confessing our sins when we commit them. But the church is wrong when it makes confessing our sins that which is done to a priest so that we can receive absolution, and it is wrong when it makes our salvation depend on this process. Yes, we must agree with God that we have sinned and ask Christ's Spirit to help us live more holy lives, but we make our confession directly to our merciful God and Father, and we do that most often in the privacy of our personal prayers. The Bible does not support the notion that we can be saved only if we are in a state of grace, as the Roman Church defines that state as the state which results when the priest absolves us of our sin in response to our confession.

I now know that the good works Christians do are not the cause of their salvation, but they are the fruit of their salvation. Those who are saved by grace alone discover that their salvation opens up an entirely new way of life for them. Their lives change. They discover that the sins that used to tempt them, don't tempt them any longer, at least not in the way they did before. The Apostle Paul says that when we are saved by the Holy Spirit's work within us, we have "died to sin." He tells us that faith in Christ means that we have died with Christ and have been raised with him so that we "may live a new life." (Romans 6:2-4) Believers do good works because they have new life in Christ, they do not do good works so that they will earn new life in Christ.

The key idea is this: *works of faith are not the cause of salvation but the result of salvation.* Salvation is impossible with man but it is possible with God. (Mark 10:27)

Because salvation gives birth to a new life, there are countless statements in the Bible that call us to live the way God wants us to live. One of the most striking is Philippians 2:12-13 where the Apostle says: "Continue to work out your salvation with fear and trembling, for it is God who works in you to will and to act according to his good purpose." The Apostle says this after he said, a few sentences earlier, "that he who began a good work in you will carry it on to completion until the day of Christ." (Philippians 1:6) The Apostle knew that the salvation of the Philippians was not dependent on their work but on the gracious work of God who would certainly carry it to completion until the very "day of Christ" when we will all appear before the throne of judgment. We need not work *for* our salvation, but we need to *work our salvation out.* That is, God has provided everything for our salvation and now he expects us to use all that he has provided to live as he wants us to live. And notice, that, even as we are told to do this, we are also told that it is God and God alone who provides the very will and energy required for this way of life.

In other words, our salvation is from God, and what we do with the grace he has given us is from God as well. We have nothing to boast about. Instead of a spirit of self-congratulation, those who are saved are overwhelmed by gratitude to God for all he has done for them through the Son of his love, Jesus.

Those who know they have been saved by grace—by grace alone through faith, not of works so that they cannot boast—discover a new excitement in their lives: they are energized by the Holy Spirit and their lives are infused with divine power. They discover that they are able to resist temptation as never before. They discover that they are able to accept the conditions of their lives, no matter what pain and sorrow they must bear. They echo what the Apostle himself said when he exclaimed: "I can do everything through him who gives me strength." (Philippians 4:13) Christ gave him his strength each day.

The Apostle Paul often speaks about the grace of God he has received through his salvation enabling him to live strenuously for God. He often compares living the new life in Christ to running a race. Writing in an environment in which people were excited about the Olympic foot races, he often used figures of speech drawn from the world of sport to show what it was like to be a Christian who had been saved by God's grace and who had, as a result, become a new creation in Christ—"the old has gone, the new has come!" (2 Corinthians 5:17)

He urges believers, "Run in such a way as to get the prize. Everyone who competes in the games goes into strict training. They do it to get a crown that will not last; but we do it to get a crown that will last forever." (1 Corinthians

9:24-25) Those who have been saved by grace and not by works do not retreat into a life of self-indulgence; on the contrary, they are swept up into the excitement of the Christian life as the Holy Spirit works in them each day.

Grace is for forever: by God's grace, believers may know right now, today, that their salvation is secure. It is there for them now, and when they die they will enter into the glory of heaven. And the grace of God is for the here and the now. As we have already noticed: "If anyone is in Christ, he is a new creation...." (2 Corinthians 5:17) Great life-changing, attitude-changing events occur in the hearts of believers, but they are not saved because of these new realities. They are saved only through the finished work of Christ. We do not have to work *for* our salvation, but once we are saved, *we work out our/ salvation*, using all the good grace God has given us so that we may serve him more effectively and more joyfully.

It is blessed relief to have our salvation removed from our own hands and placed solely in the hands of Christ. Conversion is seeing with blinding clarity that "Jesus paid it all"—he did everything necessary for our salvation. The sad reality of the Roman Church is that people like me and many of my friends who remain bound to this church can easily receive the impression that their salvation depends on their spiritual activity that gives them merit.

A prominent leader of the Protestant Reformation, John Calvin, long thought that his salvation depended on his works rather than on God's grace. In his *Commentary on the Psalms*, written in 1557, he writes: "And at first, whilst I remained thus so obstinately addicted to the superstitions of the papacy that it would have been hard indeed to have pulled me out of so deep a quagmire by sudden conversion, [God] subdued and made teachable a heart which, for my age, was far too hardened in such matters." Calvin clearly saw that he had to surrender fully to Christ and put Jesus on the throne of his life. He writes: "Never will we glory enough in Him, unless we dethrone all glory in ourselves."

The Apostle Paul, whose writing God used so powerfully in my life, had to be crushed by the glory of God when Jesus appeared to him on the road to Damascus before he realized that salvation is not based on the works we do but only on the work of Christ who paid for believers' sin when he died on the cross and rose victoriously from the dead. God chose this crushed and broken man as the instrument who proclaimed salvation based only on the finished work of Christ and not on the works of the law. Martin Luther and John Calvin, along with Scotland's John Knox and many others had the same experience: God entered their hearts through the Holy Spirit and crushed their pride; in its place, he enabled them to see that they were saved solely through the blood of Jesus.

John Woodbridge, a noted student of the Reformation period when there was a rediscovery of salvation by grace alone, marvels at what happened in John Calvin's life. Woodbridge writes: "The theo-centrism of Calvin's view of conversion is simply breathtaking. God alone is the author of our salvation. This truth crushes any vain confidence we may have mustered that our own 'righteousness' serves as the grounds for our salvation. This truth is diametrically opposed to any religious system that enshrines the teaching that we earn our salvation through our 'works' and 'merits'."

I realize that this is somewhat scholarly language, but I know what this language means because I discovered the centrality of the grace of God myself when God invaded my life with his grace and enabled me to see the light. It takes a supernatural act of Christ's Spirit to shake a stubborn person like myself free from the thought that I had something to do with earning my salvation. As a devout Roman Catholic, I truly believed that if I confessed my sins to a priest, if I went to Mass regularly (actually the more the better) and if I earnestly tried to do my best, I had a reasonably good chance of making it into heaven.

Through God's grace, I saw that my works are contaminated and feeble. I saw that my problem was much more profound than I had ever imagined. I was born separated from God and by nature I was prone to commit any and every sin. Without Christ, I was under a horrible curse that only he could remove. I began to see how rebellious I was. By nature, I resisted the good news that God had saved me through Christ alone. I was too proud to realize that I didn't have at least some role to play in earning my salvation.

Once I realized that it was true that "God so loved the world that he gave his one and only Son, that whoever believes in him shall not perish but have eternal life," (John 3:16), I humbled myself beneath his loving grace and realized that I was home free. Christ had saved me. What I could never do for myself, he did for me one hundred percent.

And then, wonder of wonders, I began to see my entire life change through the Holy Spirit's work in my heart. I realized that God's grace is for forever...and it's for now!

X

MAN-MADE RELIGION

As I look back on the way my life changed when I began to watch the television program *Faith 20*, I realize that one of the greatest barriers that confronted me as I thought about leaving Roman Catholicism was the enormity of the impression the church had made on me. Who was I to question a religion that claimed to go back to the apostles?

Who was I to question a religion that my parents and all of my relatives embraced? Who was I to question a religion that was clearly the most dominant form of Christianity in the world? Though it was true that the material I was introduced to on the *Faith 20* television program interested me greatly, it seemed presumptuous for me to question the authority of this mighty church.

Once you are accustomed to the rites and rituals of Roman Catholicism, there is something bland about most forms of Protestantism. The preacher in the Christian Reformed Church I attend wears ordinary clothing when he conducts worship on Sunday, and sometimes in the summer he doesn't wear a coat or tie. The Roman Church is overpowering. In the church I attend now there is nothing that comes anywhere near the solemnity and drama of Rome.

So, whatever would justify turning away from an extraordinarily impressive church to churches that are more common and ordinary? Of course, there are some former Roman Catholics who simply became tired of all the smells and bells of their parents' church and making the break isn't hard for them. Many of them have stopped attending church, and they don't miss the church they used to be part of. But I was a devout person, deeply impressed by church teaching and ritual, and I had to face these questions: Could a church that had been "successful" for twenty centuries be wrong? Could so many popes and other members of the teaching church be wrong?

As I pondered these questions, I gradually came to see that many of the teachings of the Roman Catholic Church contradicted the Bible even though the church is as powerful and as impressive as it is, and in spite of the fact that so many people believe what the church teaches. As I studied the Bible, I found the explanation for the fact that Roman Catholicism is as dominant as it is.

When we read the Bible, we discover that there is a simplicity in the way of salvation. The apostle Paul once answered a very distraught man who called out, "What must I do to be saved?" by saying: "Believe in the Lord Jesus Christ and you will be saved, you and your household." (Acts 16:31) Another time, he described the way of salvation this way:

"If you confess with your mouth, 'Jesus is Lord,' and believe in your heart that God raised him from the dead, you will be saved. For it is with your heart that you believe and are justified, and it is with your mouth that you confess and are saved." (Romans 10:9-10) In the same passage—Romans 10—he quotes what the Apostle Peter said on Pentecost: "Everyone who calls on the name of the Lord will be saved." (Romans 10:13)

Sinners are called to turn away from their sins, confess them to God, express their deep sorrow and ask God to help them live a holy life.

But, human nature being what it is, people are not satisfied with simplicity in religion. A great leader of the

Protestant movement in the sixteenth century—John Calvin—declared that the human heart is an idol factory. When you examine the religions of the world and when you study the history of various kinds of religion, you discover two things: (1) human creativity operates most powerfully in the realm of religion and (2) religion provides people with opportunity to exert power over one another.

The classic biblical passage that describes the way human beings pervert religion is Romans 1:18-25. As I began to understand what this passage was saying, I began to understand how it is possible for people to invent so many forms of religion, and I saw how it happened that the Christianity that started out pure in the age of the Apostles could be corrupted by human additions. This is what this passage says:

The wrath of God is being revealed from heaven against all the godlessness and wickedness of men who suppress the truth by their wickedness, since what may be known about God is plain to them, because God has made it plain to them. For since the creation of the world God's invisible qualities—his eternal power and divine nature—have been clearly seen, being understood from what has been made, so that men are without excuse.

For although they knew God, they neither glorified him as God nor gave thanks to him, but their thinking became futile and their foolish hearts were darkened. Although they claimed to be wise, they became fools and exchanged the glory of the immortal God for images made to look like mortal man and birds and animals and reptiles.

Therefore God gave them over in the sinful desires of their hearts to sexual impurity for the degrading of their bodies with one another. They exchanged the truth of God for a lie, and worshiped and served created things rather than the Creator—who is forever praised.

This passage explains why human beings are as religious as they are: God's eternal power and divinity are clearly displayed in creation, and no normal person can escape the conclusion that there must be a divine power that has made all things. Instead of worshiping the great, unseen Creator of all, human beings make idols instead. These were often represented by images of men and women and of animals. The visible, material representations of God and his power exist because people use their creativity to create substitutes that enable them to ignore the true God, who has created all things. This is as sinful as sin can be. The result of this process is that human beings who have been created in the image of God will worship, will venerate, will bow down and perform other religious acts before idols and images that are unworthy of their attention.

The Bible itself describes the way this process corrupted God's own people. Before Moses came down from the mountain where he received the perfect law of God, the people he had led out of Egypt worshiped a golden calf. Their worship was complete with all the dancing and sexual immorality that was characteristic of such worship. (Exodus 32) Their frequent descent into idol worship is documented as the Old Testament unfolds, and eight hundred years later the prophet Jeremiah wrote this word of the Lord: "What fault did your fathers find in me, that they strayed so far from me? They followed worthless idols and became worthless themselves." (Jeremiah 2:5)

Yes, it is true: the human heart is an idol factory. Just because a certain form of religion is impressive, or dominant, or influential, does not mean that it is true. All religion that is the result of the perverse human tendency to worship the creature rather than the Creator is worthless, and those who follow it will themselves become worthless. (Jeremiah 2:5)

Nowhere does the worship of the creature rather than the Creator come to greater expression than it does when religious leaders create traditions. In addition to making idols of wood and stone, the history of religion records the ability of the human mind to create rules and laws that are imposed on people so that they will be safe from damnation, at least so they are told. The Bible also provides a record of the way this process corrupted the very people of God.

The gospel of Matthew tells how the religious leaders of the Jewish people—the Pharisees and the teachers of the law— came to Jesus and complained that his disciples were breaking the tradition of the elders by not washing properly before they ate. Jesus responded by quoting the prophet Isaiah who had written this about eight hundred years earlier: "These people honor me with their lips, but their hearts are far from me. They worship me in vain; their teachings are but rules taught by men." (Isa. 29:13; Mat.15:7)

Human beings are masters at creating traditions. Some families have Christmas traditions that must be kept every year because they have been doing so for the last 35 years. (One family I know simply must put up an elaborate model train set every year at Christmas time even though no one really enjoys it that much any more.) The human tradition creating ability is nowhere more dominant than in religion. If a church has made a mistake for fifty years it becomes a tradition, and if it continues to make it for another fifty years it becomes a sacred tradition.

Some traditions are innocent, and following them makes our lives more comfortable and relieves us of having to make many small decisions. Some traditions are fun and harmless. But the traditions that grow up in a religious system are dangerous because they are able to take the place of God. Jesus rebuked the traditions of the Pharisees because they short-circuited true religion and substituted a false religion for the way of salvation. When we evaluate the Roman Catholic Church, we must be aware that that church has specifically recognized tradition as a primary component of the religious system it promotes. Its latest Catechism places what the church calls "Sacred Tradition" next to "Sacred Scripture." The Catechism declares: "Both Scripture and Tradition must be accepted and honored with equal sentiments of devotion and reverence." (82) I do not want to simplify the church's teaching regarding tradition, but this statement should alert us to the fact that there are bound to be many elements of church teaching that exist, not because they are supported by Scripture but because they are supported by tradition.

The Roman Church's insistence that tradition is as important as the Scripture itself is bound to be further established under Pope Benedict XVI, who, as Cardinal Ratzinger was one of the main authors of Rome's latest catechism that calls the church to view tradition with high reverence. His biographer, John Allen, was quoted in *U.S. News and World Report* (May 2, 2005) as stating: "In 1966 Ratzinger wanted to recover the role of Scripture as a tool for assessing church teaching and practice." The magazine then states: "By 1997, however, he warned that the use of Scripture to evaluate church teaching 'was one of the most dangerous currents to flow out of Vatican II."

Human creativity operates powerfully in the realm of religion: this is manifested in the creation of idols, some of which are material, while other idols exist in the realm of ideas in the form of rules and traditions. This is a very big subject, and what I have written about it by no means begins to exhaust it. I do not want to say that everything about the Roman Catholic Church is idolatrous and false. But once you become aware of the human ability to create false religion, you realize that just because a religion is widespread and dominant does not mean that it is true. In fact, sadly, it must be said that most religion in this world is false. As Jesus put it: "Enter through the narrow gate. For wide is the gate and broad is the road that leads to destruction, and many enter through it. But small is the gate and narrow the road that leads to life, and only a few find it." (Matthew 7:13)

Human beings tend to be creative when it comes to religion and they prefer to worship the products of their creativity rather than the only true God and his Son, the Lord Jesus Christ. And there is something else that we learn when we study worldwide religion and religion throughout the centuries: human beings use religion to exert power over one another.

Now, the desire of human beings to control others is a dark, evil power within our race. There are proper expressions of authority within human society. The Bible itself calls Christian citizens to honor the government. (1 Peter 2:13-14) There are also authority structures in the family and marriage. (Exodus 20:12; Ephesians 5:22-24) But people use money and privilege and religion to exercise power over one another. Religious power is most powerful, and throughout the ages, in every society there have been religious leaders who have used it ruthlessly.

The Bible provides a classic description of this power in the development of the Pharisee sect within the Hebrew nation. The Pharisees supplemented the true law of God with more than 600 laws they had created themselves. They spent a great deal of time checking to see whether people were obeying these laws. The laws that had to do with washing that I noted above are an example of the way the Pharisees handled the law. They followed Jesus around throughout his ministry checking on whether or not he kept the laws they had dreamed up; they were especially angry about the ways he broke the Sabbath laws that they had created. Because of the complex legal system they had made, they presented themselves as superior religious teachers whom the rest of the people was obligated to obey.

When a class of religious leaders succeeds in convincing a group of followers that they must follow their commands in order to be saved, they establish ultimate power over other people. They claim the right to control their lives in the present so that their followers will be assured of eternal life. Those who present themselves as religious leaders who have the right to tell others how to live today so that they will live forever have the strongest leadership position there is.

Once a class of people achieve this ultimate power over others, they refuse to let it go. Islam is an example of the way this operates. Islam is a religion in which many leaders exercise life and death power over their followers. What we see clearly in Islam is an element of all religion. Religious leaders always want to exercise power. This is why religious leaders are very dangerous people. As I began to look at the Roman Catholic Church objectively, I began to realize that the church had developed an enormous power structure that is virtually impossible to withstand, especially when you are part of the religious system yourself. When you take the great power of tradition within the church and combine that with the church's highly organized power structure, you find yourself dealing with a formidable force.

I began this chapter noting that that initially I had felt very uneasy leaving a church that I long believed it to be the one and only true church of Jesus Christ. I began to realize that over the centuries, the Roman Church had built effective components into its structure that made it virtually impossible to question its teaching.

What the church has done is create a church structure that creates a fundamental division within it that automatically disqualifies any objection brought against its doctrines. If anyone or any group of believers raises questions about its teaching, these objections are viewed as improper from the outset because church teaching is not to be questioned by those outside the teaching church. Indeed, in my youth, had I questioned or otherwise doubted church doctrine even if only in my mind, I considered it heretical and Satan's doing and quickly cast away such thoughts.

From time to time, the teaching church itself may examine and evaluate Roman Catholic practices, but a person like me has no standing whatsoever if I raise any questions or doubts.

The division that the Roman Church has created within itself, puts the teaching church (which I just mentioned) on one side of the divide and the laity on the other side of the divide.

When I would bring up some of my problems with the church in conversation with other Roman Catholics, they would remind me that raising such questions was none of my business. I was a member of the lay church—I was not a part of the teaching church. The teaching church (which sanctioned the sacrament of holy orders) is made up of those who read the Bible, study it, and who know about what they call Sacred Tradition. And it is this part of the church that is in charge of determining what is proper church doctrine. Lay members of the church, such as I used to be, should only follow the leading of their priests. It is through the local priest that the lay members receive two very important things: absolution from their sin and the teaching that they need to embrace. The priest, clearly, has a strangle hold on local believers. It is true, of course, that all believing communities have certain people who tend to teach other members what they need to know. A pastor in a Protestant Church is a teacher, and if a church is any size at all, there will be other believers who have the gift of teaching, and churches use these people in their ministries. But the teaching element of the Roman Church is different from the way the gift of teaching is exercised in the church I now attend. The teaching element of the Roman Church is based on its view of the role of the apostles in the church's life. It's worth looking at closely.

First of all, we must recognize that the apostles had an extremely important role in the church. I am always impressed when I read Revelation 21:14 that describes the New Jerusalem (the church) coming down from heaven this way: "The wall of the city had twelve foundations, and on them were the names of the twelve apostles of the Lamb." In our church, we often confess our faith by using the well-known Apostles' Creed. Occasionally, we use the Nicene Creed when we confess our faith, and that creed has this in it: "I believe one holy catholic and apostolic Church." The word *catholic* in this statement means *universal*, not *Roman*

Catholic. Just now, I want to call attention to the word *apostolic*. We believe the church is apostolic in the sense that Christ appointed his apostles to represent him in their teaching, and he promised them the Holy Spirit who would lead them into all truth. (John 16:13-15). Their teaching has been preserved for us in the New Testament Scriptures. Ephesians 2:20 says that the church is built on the foundation of the "apostles and the prophets, with Christ Jesus himself as the chief cornerstone."

The Roman Catholic Church has taken the biblical teaching regarding the importance of the apostles and given it their own spin. The church centers the biblical doctrine of the apostolicity of the church in the Apostle Peter, whom they consider the primary apostle. They base this on Matthew 16 where Peter answers Jesus' question, "who do you say that I am?" with the declaration, "You are the Christ, the Son of the living God." Jesus responded to Peter's statement this way: "Blessed are you, Simon son of Jonah, for this was not revealed to you by flesh and blood but by my Father in heaven. And I tell you that you are Peter, and on this rock I will build my church, and the gates of Hades will not overcome it."

That is a very impressive statement, but it cannot by used to support the primacy of the papacy. When Jesus spoke of Peter's "rock function" he was not speaking of the role of his person, but was referring to the clear statement Peter had just made, under the influence of the Holy Spirit, that Jesus of Nazareth was the Christ, the Son of the living God. Though the rest of the New Testament shows that Peter had an important role in the life of the church, it is a great leap to the conclusion that church doctrine through the years has come to us and will continue to come to us from Peter's throne in Rome. This issue is worth discussing in far greater detail than I am able to do here, but anyone who knows Peter's story that followed his confession knows that it was somewhat checkered.

The church is apostolic but its apostolicity is rooted in the perfection of the Scriptures that the prophets of the Old Testament and the apostles of the new have given us. Today, the church advances in the truth if it is bound to the biblical testimony. The Bible alone is our only rule for faith and life. A teaching church, centered in the pope in Rome, is not our rule for faith and life. Over the years there have been many teachings that have come from the Rome's Holy See that are good and useful, but they have not been this way because of their origin but rather because they are supported by Scripture. But many of the teachings have no moral authority whatsoever because they are rooted in what is called Sacred Tradition that often contradicts the Bible itself.

As a devout Roman Catholic, all of this was completely out of my field of vision. I had no idea that the church I was part of built many of its teachings on material taken from tradition rather than the Bible. When these teachings are presented to you by a person clothed in priestly vestments and when it is all accompanied by the powerful ritual and religious pageantry of the church, and when your family and friends remind you that you are not to question what the church teaches you, you just accept what you are told.

Besides, I had no clue about the way religious leaders use their so-called "spiritual" power to create positions of enormous natural power for themselves. I did not see how the Roman way of salvation contributed to the church's amassing unimaginable power in the lives of those who longed for salvation. So I was locked in for life, at least I would have been if I had not been turned aside by biblical truth I had never known before.

The first thing I began to see was that the way of salvation described in the Bible is not the same as that described by the church. I began to understand that the Bible tells us about a way of salvation that is from God from beginning to end. Our works have nothing whatsoever to do with the righteousness we need if we are going to be saved.

Our righteousness is from God alone, through grace. Salvation is through amazing grace, not grace plus works. Once I began to see that the church was seriously wrong in its teaching about salvation, I began to go deeper, to read and study more. Among other things, I learned what happened at the time of the Protestant Reformation.

It was Martin Luther who saw the fundamental Roman error regarding salvation, and God used him to help many see the truth about salvation. So the Reformation began. When this man, an Augustinian monk and professor of theology, saw that salvation is through faith alone, not of works, he took his stand against the papacy. He discovered that Peter, like all the other apostles, and like all of us today, was a seriously flawed person. True, his confession of Christ as the Son of God was extremely significant, but before the conversation with Christ that included that confession was ended, he opposed Christ's mission so vehemently that Christ had to say: "Get behind me, Satan! You are a stumbling block to me; you do not have in mind the things of God, but the things of men." (Matthew 16:23) Peter himself had to reprimand a Roman centurion named Cornelius who fell at his feet in an attitude of worship; Peter said: "Stand up, I am only a man myself." (Acts 10:26) The Apostle Paul had to reprimand Peter because Peter was not acting in line with the gospel message. Galatians 2:11-14 preserves a detailed description of the way Paul finally had to oppose Peter to his face "because he was clearly in the wrong." No, the Bible does not support the notion that Peter became the primary source of church teaching and the pope is Peter's successor who has been the last word on church teaching and remains the same today.

At the Synod of Jerusalem, Peter made an important speech that contributed to the synod's progress, but when the synod was over, it was the Lord's brother James who issued the statement that represented the Holy Spirit-led wisdom and judgment of the entire assembly. (See Acts 15:1-22)

When we read the record of that synod, we observe that Paul and Barnabas also contributed to the decision. The Bible does not support the Roman Catholic hierarchical structure, with the pope, supposedly representing Peter, at the top, and with all of the rest of the teaching church ranged below him, the parish priest representing this massive human construction on the local level. All this is an extremely effective way to maintain a hold on the ordinary people of the congregations, but it is a man-made approach.

As I began to see these things, I realized that just because a church boasts so big a following and has a long history, does not mean that it is what God wants the church to be and that it is what I need as a sinner desperately in need of salvation. If you are where I was several years ago, accepting the church's teaching without question, I earnestly invite you to think deeply about where you are in your spiritual life. It is not true that the Roman Catholic Church is the only body that is qualified to teach ordinary men and women what they need to know in order to be saved. In fact, if you are going to experience the glorious benefits that we have when we discover the way of salvation by grace alone, through faith alone, based on the Bible alone, you will have to disentangle yourself from this massive church.

My prayer is that what I am sharing with you will set you thinking deeply about your own spiritual life and your own salvation. My prayer is that you will find your way into a church where the Bible is the only authority for faith and life, where Christ is exalted and where worship is unencumbered by complicated ritual. There are churches like that. I know. I have found such a church and my life has been elevated to new levels of joy. But, please, let me tell you more.

XI

LEAVING MARY

Whenever you make a big move from one place to another or from one job to another, it's always difficult leaving friends behind. Oh, that doesn't mean that you never see them again, but once you have formed a pattern that daily includes your friends and then you don't see them very much any more, something like grief takes over inside you. When this happens, we don't usually think of the twinges of feeling we experience as *grief,* but it is something like that.

Well, there is something like that that happens when a devout Roman Catholic as I was moves out of the church into a church that feels different, acts different, looks different and even smells different. All these differences require adjustment that takes time. But, along with these differences, when you leave the Roman Church that has formed you on the deepest levels, you also leave people who have been important to you.

When a serious believer leaves Rome, he also leaves a multitude of people whom the church insists are helpful in our life of grace. They are those elevated to sainthood who now populate heaven's courts prepared to assist us earthlings by praying for us and, supposedly, giving our prayers a special weight by their endorsement of our requests.

It wasn't that I was afraid to come directly into God's presence with my prayers, but when you have those who are in heaven who will give your prayers a boost, it's nice to use them sometime. I am thankful that once I saw the full picture of salvation and the fact that the saints have no role in securing mine, it was easy for me to set them aside and pray to God solely through Jesus Christ my Savior..

Of all the glorified saints, of course, Mary, Jesus' mother according to the flesh, is the most prominent and powerful, and leaving her is not easy. Not until you realize what has happened in the Roman Church's centuries-long promotion of Mary are you able to remove her entirely from your heart. The tie between individual Roman Catholic believers and Mary is deeply emotional. It involves many layers of attachment. In Roman Catholicism, the supreme effectiveness of Mary's role in redemption is no more questioned than the role of Christ himself. When someone does question the exaltation of Mary over the centuries, it is often viewed as blasphemy.

Mary's place in Roman Catholicism is doubly powerful. She represents a feminine principle in the faith, and all non-biblical religion requires this. The pantheon of deities found among the Romans and the Greeks included powerful goddesses. And a cursory examination of most non-Christian religions will reveal strong elements of the feminine, in some of them to the point of the erotic. Mary's role, however, transcends the provision of a feminine principle.

Mary's is also a major element in the development of the *gratia cooperans* teaching that Rome has developed. When I was a Roman Catholic I didn't think about grace a great deal in connection with salvation, but when I did connect the two I naturally figured that we were required to cooperate with God in our salvation. In this view, the work of God in salvation, especially in the great sacrifice of Christ, is primary, but the work of man enters into the picture as well. God does his part and man must do his. The regimen of works required to assure us that our crimes and misdemeanors are forgiven is the most prominent example of the salvation obligations the church lays on its members.

Go to confession, tell your sins to a priest, and be sure to fully recite whatever prayer penance you're given. The good works you perform later on will make you more pleasing to God and this would likely help reduce the length of your final purification stint in purgatory.

The Church also teaches that Mary played a major role in establishing this formula for salvation. When the angel Gabriel appeared to her and explained the marvel of the virgin birth to her, she responded, "I am the Lord's servant. May it be to me as you have said." In the church's presentation of Mary, that statement of unconditional obedience has become unusually important. Because it says when Mary agreed to bear Jesus, the Son of God, she established the principle of man's cooperation with God in the salvation process. Therefore, God's use of Mary and her willingness to be used by God shows in the most dramatic way possible that salvation without human assistance is impossible. God needs man in order to save man.

Rome says Mary's willingness to be used the way she was is the highest level of human obedience imaginable, and her total submission to the will of God has made her worthy of the honor and the trust of ordinary people who will never have the opportunity to serve God to the extent that she did.

Because Mary provides a powerful feminine element in Roman Catholic religion along with the more theological element that supports the idea that saving grace has both a divine and a human element, it is not hard to understand her dominant role in the faith. It is no wonder that she is revered, honored, venerated, even worshiped, by some. The very idea that anyone would question the propriety of praying to her, or at least praying through her to her Son Jesus, is considered by devote Roman Catholics as the depth of impiety.

In fact, the role of Mary in the church is so dominant and so contrary to Protestantism that the idea of leaving the church and abandoning the Holy Mother is so abhorrent to many Roman Catholics that they cannot even imagine leaving the church in which Mary plays such an important role. The other side of this is that the idea of venerating Mary is so foreign to many Protestants that many of them feel awkward, even embarrassed, when they think of the possibility of praying to God through Mary, and this, if nothing else, keeps them from considering the Roman Church (or the Orthodox Church for that matter) as an option.

I moved away from Mary decisively when I realized that the Roman teaching regarding her was a human fabrication. Since the seventh century, the church has moved steadily in the direction of making her so essential for the achievement of salvation that she has become a co-mediator with her Son Jesus.

In their book *Roman Catholics and Evangelicals,* Norman Geisler and Ralph E. MacKenzie provide the documentation for what I found to be true about Mary. The church has made teachings regarding her person and her work to be part of church doctrine though they have no foundation in the Scriptures. They are in fact refuted by the Scripture. This is what they are.

First of all, I learned that the church's teaching regarding the perpetual virginity of Mary was without Biblical support. The Bible declares that Jesus was conceived in Mary's womb without Joseph or any other male. Mary was a virgin when she conceived Jesus and when she carried him. The Roman Church further holds that she had no other children. This adamant insistence on her virginity arises from the church's assumption that ordinary sexual activity of a man and woman in marriage is inferior to the state of virginity. The Bible does not support this. Genesis 2:18-25 reveals that God realized that it was not good that man should be alone, and so he created a woman for him who became his wife: the two became one flesh. It shows that marriage, with the marital intimacies that characterize it, is as pure and chaste as singleness and provides both partners with fulfillment that enhances their character and personality.

In keeping with this biblical view of marriage, the Bible reports that Mary had the usual life of a married woman with children after she gave birth to Jesus. In addition to the Bible's use of normal language to describe Jesus' birth, several passages in the Synoptic gospels show us that Jesus had brothers and sisters. Matthew 13:55-56 specifically mentions Jesus' siblings. Here we find a record of the people's puzzled response to Jesus' miracles and authoritative speech; they asked: "Isn't this the carpenter's son? Isn't his mother's name Mary, and aren't his brothers James, Joseph, Simon and Judas? Aren't all his sisters with us?" Roman Catholic teaching declares that these brothers and sisters were cousins, but there is nothing in the words employed that supports this; Scripture leaves no room for doubt as to whether Mary had other children. "I saw none of the other apostles–only James, the Lord's brother. (Galatians 1:19) "I am a stranger to my brothers, an alien to my own mother's sons." (Psalm 69:8).

Though Joseph was the adoptive father of Jesus and not his natural father, he was most certainly the natural father of Jesus' brothers and sisters, and they were his wife Mary's children. The Bible actually tells us that, though Joseph had no sexual union with his wife before the birth of Jesus, he did afterward: Matthew 1:25 says, "He had no union with her until she gave birth to a son."

That the church continues to perpetuate the idea of Mary's perpetual virginity in direct contradiction of biblical statements is a serious rejection of biblical authority. Once I began to see that, I realized that what I had been taught about Mary was not bringing me closer to God but leading me further away from him.

But there is more to the church's teaching about her. In 1854, Pope Pius X declared in a papal bull called *Ineffabilis* that Mary's own conception occurred in such a way that she herself was without sin. The main support for this astounding teaching as that it had been revealed by God to the teaching church apart from the Bible, and was, consequently, an obligatory belief for all the faithful. To suggest that the biblical statements brought forward to support this teaching come anywhere near doing so requires switching our minds to off. The two statements in Luke that call Mary blessed (1:28 and 42) do not say that Mary is blessed *above* women, but *among* them. There is no question that she was blessed, and we may call her the "blessed virgin" still today. But that is a far cry from saying that she was sinless like her Son. Since the Fall of Adam into sin, only one person has ever been without sin and that was Jesus Christ, who was born of Mary, according to the flesh.

In the song that Mary voiced immediately after her cousin Elizabeth called her "blessed among women," Mary acknowledged that she needed a Savior. She said: "My soul glorifies the Lord and my spirit rejoices in God my Savior, for he is mindful of the humble state of his servant."

She continues and says that all generations will call her blessed, but she clearly realized that she was a sinner who needed God's saving work if she were to be saved.

As I realized that it was simply untrue that Mary had been conceived in such a way that she was sinless and pure, I realized how the church had been leading me along a dark and dangerous path. And I saw that also in connection with other alleged truths about Mary not supported by the Bible.

Another church teaching that has no Biblical foundation and very little other support, is the doctrine of Mary's alleged sinlessness. This teaching is possible because of the prior declaration that Mary was conceived without being contaminated by original sin. Building on the dogma of the Immaculate Conception, the church declared that Mary escaped the contamination of ordinary sin; this was declared by the Council of Trent that was convened in response to the threat to the church posed by the Protestant Reformation.

The Biblical foundation for this teaching is supposed to be Gabriel's greeting when he announced the miracle of the virgin birth to her, "Hail Mary, full of grace." The *Hailing of Mary* has become an important element in Roman liturgy and personal devotion, but it is based on a faulty translation of the Greek original. The hailing of Mary and the statement about her "fullness of grace" is based on a the Latin Vulgate version of the Bible, and the modern Catholic Bible now corrects the reading so that Mary is called the "favored one," instead of "full of grace." There is a vast difference between these, as you can see. If you are *full* of grace, there is no room for any "un-grace," or sin. There is no reason to suppose that Mary was sinless, even though she was highly favored.

Interestingly, the support for this teaching among the church fathers is also very thin. Surprisingly, Thomas Aquinas, who rejected the teaching of the Immaculate Conception, nevertheless affirmed Mary's sinlessness—a remarkably confused position for a theologian whose precision and logic is otherwise exemplary.

But there is more. A person, perpetually virgin, herself immaculately conceived and sinless is surely a candidate for a special entrance into heaven. So after all of this, it is no surprise that in 1950 the church spoke *ex cathedra* that "just as the glorious resurrection of Christ was an essential part, and final evidence of the victory, so the Blessed Virgin's common struggle with her son was to be concluded with the 'glorification' of her virginal body."

The church went on to announce that in Mary's bodily assumption into heaven, she "finally attained as the highest crown of her privileges, that she should be immune from the corruption of the tomb, and that in the same manner as her Son she would overcome death and be taken away soul and body to the supernatural glory of heaven, where as Queen she would shine forth at the right hand of the same Son of hers, the Immortal King of Ages."

But there is nothing in Scripture that supports the bodily assumption of Mary into heaven. Here again, we see how Rome leads its faithful to embrace a teaching that the Bible does not support. But really that does not make a great deal of difference because the certainty of this alleged exaltation of Mary does not rest on the Bible but on the teaching power of the church. As a Roman Catholic I could never consider questioning a teaching from Rome that I faithfully considered a divine revelation through Christ's representative on earth – the Pope. After all, I believed the spiritual leader of the Roman Catholic Church would be the best person to teach me the Word of God in the Bible. And the church, when it teaches, takes the Bible seriously, but also tradition and then, along with both of these together, relies on what it considers its prerogative to announce new teaching as it did in this case, a bit more than a half century ago.

With all of this, it is no wonder that for Roman Catholics, Mary now occupies a role of mediator between ordinary believers and God. Since the fifteenth century, Mary has been called the Co-redemptrix along with her Son, though this has not yet been incorporated into dogma. When you examine the language used to describe the nature of her work, it is full of statements that emphasize Christ's primary role in redemption, but attached to such statements are descriptions of Mary's importance that cause her to be viewed as virtually equal to Jesus in the minds of garden-variety Roman Catholics. In my case, for example, as a devout member of the church, for all practical purposes Mary was as important for salvation as Jesus, though in another way.

An example of the way Mary's role in salvation is described is this statement made by Pope Leo XIII: "Nothing whatever of that immense treasure of all graces, which the Lord brought us...is granted to us, *save through Mary*, (emphasis mine) so that, just as no one can come to the Father on high except through the Son, so almost in the same manner, no one can come to Christ except through his

Mother." When the Roman Church deals with 1 Timothy 2:5 (*There is one God and one mediator between God and men, the man Christ Jesus....*) it acknowledges the primary role of Christ as mediator, but then, in the words of Thomas Aquinas, immediately adds: "But there is nothing to prevent others in a certain way (*secundum quid*) from being called mediators between God and man, in so far as they, by preparing or serving...co-operate in uniting men with God." It is this kind of ambiguous language that feeds the fires of Mary's exaltation.

Once I saw that my faith needed to be formed and fed by the Bible alone, I began to realize that I was being led away from the truth of God regarding salvation by these non-biblical teachings about Mary. And once I realized that Christ and Christ alone was my only hope for salvation, it troubled me to see my friends virtually worship Mary. Now, I know that if I were to talk to them about this, they would point out that they worship only God, but they venerate Mary. However, when you look closely at Roman Catholic teaching, you discover that the church encourages its members to give Mary an honor so great that it can hardly be distinguished from the honor given Mary's son.

Geisler and MacKenzie (*Roman Catholics and Evangelicals: Agreements and Differences* p. 320) point out that the church explicitly states that Mary is worthy of what is called the "cult of hyperdulia." And what is that? Well, God himself is worthy of what is called *latria*—that is the highest adoration mortals can bring. Mary is the only creature worthy of hyperdulia, and saints and angels are worthy of dulia. To be sure, the word *dulia* is not familiar to many of us, but it should be clear that the honor that Mary is entitled to receive is greater than the honor that should be given any other creature, including the archangels Gabriel and Michael.

When we examine the books that honor Mary we find prayers that clearly indicate that the supplicant views her as essential for salvation. Listen to this line from a prayer found in such a book: "Come to my aid, dearest Mother, for I recommend myself to thee. In thy hands I place my eternal salvation, and to thee I entrust my soul."

All this means that ordinary Roman Catholics like I was for many years view Mary as the key person who will insure their salvation. If Mary wants them to go to heaven, they can be sure they will go there. Many believe that God himself cannot turn away Mary's requests. She gets what she asks for. So for all practical purposes, the way the ordinary believer perceives Mary is hardly different from the way a believer perceives God. One thing is sure, according to the church, her role in making salvation possible for people like me is so great, I must make it my business to make sure that I honor her properly. That is what I believed for many years, and that is why I made sure that I said my "Hail Marys."

What is so sad about all this is that many people will pursue their salvation by leaning on Mary, and this is a fatal error. We have already noticed that it is wrong for us to depend on ourselves and our own works for our salvation— this has been one of the main points I have been making. It is just as wrong to depend on the mediatorship of another person who is no different from us in terms of her own need of salvation. As we have seen, Mary's perpetual virginity, her immaculate conception, her bodily assumption into heaven, her sinlessness and her supposed role in salvation itself cannot be supported by the Bible. People who honor Mary with something that comes very close to worship— veneration—and who depend on her to insure their entrance into heaven are actually in grave danger. What will happen to the souls of those who are trusting in even the slightest measure on another sinful human being for their salvation? What will happen to them? Their future is very grim.

Another sad result of the Roman Catholic Church's teachings about Mary is that people like me who walk away from that church often think and speak (and write) about Mary in very negative terms.

Because Rome's teaching about her is at the very least terribly misleading and at worst dreadfully sinful, we fail to appreciate the wonder and the glory of her actual role in God's salvation work.

I recognize Mary as an unusually blessed person. The privilege granted her was the highest imaginable. She was a godly person, a young woman who was apparently steeped in the Old Testament Scriptures, a thoughtful person who seems to have spent more time than Joseph meditating on the magnitude of the miracle of Christ's first coming. She figures in some of the events of Jesus' ministry itself, and when he died, she cringed as the sword of his execution pierced her heart along with his. She was part of the 120 believers who were in the room the day the Holy Spirit was poured out on the church. Believers cannot help but be deeply impressed by this faith filled sister in Christ.

She is innocent of the perpetration of all the teachings that have led people astray when they have thought about her, and I try to remind myself of the positive feelings I should have about this woman.

In my eyes, Mary stands with all the special people in the Bible—Abraham, Moses, David, Elijah, Isaiah, the apostles Peter and John and Paul, the man who walked the streets of my native Malta. And, of course, there are many more. She is among them, with Mary Magdalene, Elizabeth, Priscilla and countless others, all of whom had a role to play in God's great work of salvation. Do we honor these people? Not really. We hold them in high esteem, but mainly we thank God for giving them to us and letting them be the God-gifted people they were with a special task to perform. Yes, basically we thank God for them. But not one of these esteemed people can ever do one thing that can help us enter heaven, not one of them. And no one knows that better than Mary herself.

If this is true, how did it happen that the church teachings we have just looked at developed over the years?

This is the question that puzzled me as I began to see that the way of salvation taught by the church I had been a part of for many decades was not actually the way of salvation. When you look at the way the Marian teachings developed over the years, at the many documents that assure the faithful that she is even the Co-Mediatrix with Jesus and at the wide spread power of the Marian Cult today, with no one more supportive of the veneration than Pope John Paul II, you cannot help wonder how this great Marian doctrinal system could have developed.

Well, here is yet another example of the way human beings, by nature, will worship the creature rather than the creator, as Romans 1:25 puts it. Remember what John Calvin wrote: "The human heart is an idol factory." Human beings are geniuses when it comes to creating new religions and when it comes to adding to the true religion of the Bible. And I began to see that this deforming religious power had created the church's non-biblical emphasis on Mary. I began to realize that so long as I included her in my ideas regarding my own salvation, I was on very dangerous ground because this detracted from my understanding that my salvation depended on Christ alone from first to last.

And as I thought about all this more, I couldn't help but ask why the church had allowed this to happen. It was not a part of the earliest expressions of Christian piety. If God wanted Mary so highly revered, Scripture would have made it crystal clear.

Surely there is not the slightest hint in the New Testament that Mary had a special role in the church. The very idea that anyone would pray to her is light years removed from anything we find in the Bible. How did this happen? Why did this happen?

It has pained me to conclude that what we have here is yet another example of the deepest perversity of the human heart. Human beings love, literally love, to create religion, and when they do that they always tend to create religion that is most attractive to the masses.

As I pointed out, Roman Catholic Marian teaching provided popular religion with a feminine dimension that appealed to the common people. On the battlefield, when soldiers are mortally wounded, they often call for their mothers; well, here is a mother at the center of their religion, and they can call out to her in their distress.

The exaltation of Mary also makes heavenly reality more accessible. You don't have to go directly to God; you can pray to the Virgin and ask her to pray for you "now and in the hour of death." And when you are taught, as the church clearly teaches, that the grace of God is available to them through Mary's intercession, it makes the life of faith easier.

With this, as we have seen, the exaltation of Mary implies a role of high importance for human beings in the work of salvation. *Co-redemptress, Mediatrix*—these are extremely impressive names for another human being. Yes, God is the Savior, but he also needs the work of human beings to make salvation happen, according to Rome. This contradicts the Bible's message which tells us that with man salvation is impossible, but not with God. (Matthew 19:25-26)

You see, having Mary in this exalted role makes the Roman Catholic religion much more attractive. Allowing the teachings about her to develop through the centuries strengthened the hold of the Roman Church on its members. These teachings make the church much more powerful. One of the reasons Roman Catholicism is the first group among Christians is the attractiveness of its Marian teachings.

When teachings make a church more powerful, the church will not change them, even if they are untrue. And so throughout the centuries, one teaching about Mary built on earlier ones, and so on, until we finally have the full blown Marian system. I do not like to introduce something so common into a discussion this serious, but I think that this idea helps us understand what happened: *Make a mistake once and it's a mistake; make a mistake twice and it becomes a tradition.* Well, there is something to that. This simple statement goes far in explaining how the church's attachment to Mary developed.

So I left the Mary of Roman Catholicism, but I found the real Mary. She is a sinner as I am. She depends on Christ alone for her salvation, as I do. As I think of her role in the coming of my Savior, I honor her as one who has been blessed among women, among them, not above them. She is my sister in Christ and with her I turn my eyes on Jesus who has done everything required for my salvation.

XII

THE MASS

You may have heard that there is a Chinese proverb that goes like this: *If you want to know about water, don't ask a fish.* I must confess that I am not absolutely sure it's Chinese, but if it is, the Chinese can be proud. It makes a very good point.

The point is that fish are the last to know anything about water because they are too close to it. And as I gradually worked my way out of Roman Catholicism, I realized that I had been too close to it for years to really understand what was going on. I was reared as a devout Roman Catholic and I simply received what I was taught as true. I wasn't always thrilled about what I learned, but it never entered my mind to question it. Its priests have absolute authority regarding matters of faith. Who was I to protest?

When a person grows up like that it seems as if the entire religion forms a seamless garment that enfolds him. Because there is no distance between you and the church's teaching, you become incapable of examining what you are learning. You become like that proverbial fish who is too close to its liquid environment to raise questions about it.

As I became more and more acquainted with the man from Malta, the apostle Paul, and as I began to think more about the biblical letters he wrote, I began to realize that the Roman Church was cheating me. The church taught a way of salvation that required specific works that I had to do, whereas the apostle Paul wrote that we are saved through faith alone, apart from works. The Bible's message declares that we are saved by the blood of Christ, not by doing what the church tells us to do.

My new understanding of the way of salvation began to put some distance between me and the church, and that enabled me to see more clearly what happens to a person when he or she simply accepts what the church teaches without question. As I began to see Roman Catholic teaching more clearly, I realized that the heart of Roman Catholicism is the sacramental system.

Now, the church I am a member of (which happens to be a Christian Reformed Church) takes the sacraments very seriously, but the sacraments have an entirely different role in this evangelical Protestant Church than they have in Roman Catholicism. In the Roman Church the sacraments are absolutely necessary for salvation. Let me sketch the Roman teaching for a moment.

According to Rome, there are seven sacraments, and you had better believe that. If you believe that there are only two—Baptism and Holy Communion—as I now do, the Roman Church has said, *let him be anathema*, which means *let him be damned*. According to Rome, five of these sacraments are necessary for everyone: baptism, confirmation, Eucharist, penance, and the anointing of the sick. Two others are only for certain individuals—matrimony and holy orders. An unmarried lay person would do best to make sure that he or she has the grace that is conferred by the first five I have mentioned because they are essential for salvation.

In the Roman view the sacraments are the engines that drive the grace machine. At the major church council that was held after the Protestant Reformation, the Council of Trent, the church declared: "If anyone shall say that the sacraments of the New Law are not necessary for salvation, but are superfluous, and that, although all are not necessary individually, without them or without the desire of them through faith alone men obtain from God the grace of justification: let him be anathema."

Notice that that statement explicitly rejects the idea that we are justified by faith alone and emphatically declares that the sacraments are necessary for salvation. In this view they are necessary because they confer grace upon those who are touched by them. The sacraments act like faucets that convey grace directly to the people who receive them. And they do this automatically, regardless of the moral quality of the priests who administer them and regardless of the moral quality of the persons who receive them. The Council of Trent coined a special Latin phrase to describe the fact that grace is surely received when a person receives the sacrament: *ex opere operato*. This Latin term means that sacraments are uniquely powerful because they communicate divine grace. If a person does not receive them, that person will not be justified; that person will not be saved.

Over the centuries, the Roman Church has become an enormous institution that dispenses grace by means of the sacraments. Because of this, it can promise all who participate in the sacramental life of the church that they are pleasing God. These people do not have to know a great deal about church teaching, they do not have to be very devout churchgoers, they do not have to be very pure and holy—all they need do is confess serious sin to a priest, receive the grace that accompanies forgiveness and penance, and go to mass. If they do this, holiness will be conferred upon them and they would be pleasing to God.

When I was a Roman Catholic the heart of this entire sacramental system was the mass and the Eucharist at its center. If you are a Roman Catholic, likely the mass is the center of your church experience too. It is worth looking at the church's teaching regarding the mass because that teaching shows how the sacramental system conveys grace, and it shows that the grace that is conveyed is substantial.

When I say that grace is *substantial* in the Roman system I mean that it is like a substance that passes from the hands of the priest into the life of the communicant.

The full power of the Roman Church's sacramental system is expressed in the mass because in this sacrament, the very substance used is changed into life-giving nourishment. The church teaches that during the administration of this sacrament, the bread and wine are actually changed into the true body and blood of Christ. The defining mark of the priesthood is that those who are ordained as priests are empowered to bring about this change in ordinary bread and wine. They receive this ability as an "indelible character" that can never be erased.

It is worth going to the most recent catechism of the Roman Catholic Church to see how the mass—the celebration of what the church calls the Holy Eucharist—is the high point of the entire sacramental system. Section 1374 of the catechism states: "The mode of Christ's presence under the Eucharistic species [the bread and the wine] is unique. It raises the Eucharist above all the sacraments as 'the perfection of the spiritual life and the end to which all the sacraments tend.' In the most blessed sacrament of the Eucharist 'the body and blood, together with the soul and divinity, of our Lord Jesus Christ and, therefore, *the whole Christ is truly, really, and substantially* contained."

Because the church declares that the bread and the wine are transformed into the actual body and blood of Christ, a number of distinctively Roman Catholic events occur. First of all, at the center of the worship service is the worship of the elements themselves—the bread and the wine are considered worthy of the most profound worship.

Second, a Roman Catholic Church becomes a holy place because it houses the substance that has been transformed into Christ's body and blood. It is kept in the tabernacle near the altar, and the faithful express their worship of the holy contents on the altar by genuflecting any time they need to walk across the altar.

Third, the fact that the actual body and blood of Christ are present in each worship service makes attendance at worship a solemn obligation. When I was a Roman Catholic, I did not partake of Holy Communion each time I worshiped, but I was assured that my very presence at mass and my adoration of the sacred elements was a meritorious act.

Fourth, the fact that the bread and the wine become the true body and blood of Christ makes the mass a powerful repetition of the sacrifice of Christ. The church today denies that what happens at the mass is actually a re-doing of the crucifixion itself; they insist that Christ's crucifixion was a once-for-all event. But the church's emphasis on the reality of Christ's body in the mass supports the notion that the divine energy and forgiving grace that was released when Jesus died is expressed, re-focused and brought into play whenever the mass is offered. It is as if the crucifixion itself is actualized again.

From childhood I looked upon the "sacrifice of the mass" as an ever-continuing sin-offering of Christ's crucifixion. I recall a prayer from my youth recited during an Adoration of the Blessed Sacrament devotion at church that, in part said: "Wherein thou renew, though bloodlessly, that self-same sacrifice which thou did consummate on Calvary for our salvation."

The mass then is the center and the high point of the entire sacramental system of salvation. As the catechism says: "The mode of Christ's presence under the Eucharistic species [the bread and the wine] is unique. It raises the Eucharist above all the sacraments as 'the perfection of the spiritual life and the end to which all the sacraments tend." Virtually every element of the church's life is affected by the mass. Everything the church does circles around the mass. Take the mass out of the Roman Catholic equation and the church will disintegrate.

When you think about it, the sacramental system in general and the sacrament of the mass in particular is a source of the church's enormous power. The church encourages its members to believe that there is actually a place in this corrupt world where Christ is present still today. This presence is, according the catechism, a "presence in the fullest sense; that is, to say, it is a *substantial* presence by which Christ, God and man, makes himself wholly and entirely present." Once a person believes this, as I did for many years, attending mass becomes the primary worship event in a person's life, and receiving the consecrated Eucharist becomes an event of indescribable importance. Everything else revolves around this. The church requires that a person partake of Holy Communion at least once a year. I did it far more often than that. And I assumed that, because I did, the possibility for my salvation was heightened.

And as you may know, the power of the mass extends beyond the lives of those who partake of it in the present. The church encourages its living members to arrange for masses to be said for those who have died. These masses for the dead are supposed to confer significant benefits on the deceased. When the faithful believe that the benefits of an ecclesiastical act spill over into the eternal realm, such an act becomes enormously powerful.

This sacramental system, with the mass as its centerpiece, is yet another explanation for the Roman Church's unusual power. With such a supernatural event at its center (the alleged changing of the bread and wine into the actual body of Christ) the church's importance is imposing and overwhelming. Those who grow up in this religion cannot easily question it. Those who become converts are excited to be members of a church where they believe the actual body and blood is present.

The sacramental system gives the church a monopoly on grace. In the Roman view, grace is a substance, and this substance can enter human lives only through the ministry of the church. Grace is not available elsewhere, and since grace is necessary for salvation, the church has a strangle hold on its members. They must remain in the church to be saved. They need the Eucharist for their salvation as much as they need air to breath for their physical lives.

It grieves me to say this, but here again is another case where the church depends on falsehood in order to maintain its powerful grip on its members' lives. The fundamental flaw with regard to the church's teaching regarding the mass is that it is not supported by the Bible. It is a human fabrication to declare that the bread and the wine become the actual body of Christ and are thus worthy of worship. Admittedly, it is a very impressive teaching, even very attractive; the problem is that it is not true.

In order to support its teaching regarding the change of the water and wine into the body and blood of Christ, the church relies on what it calls the doctrine of transubstantiation. This doctrine declares that at the moment the priest consecrates the bread and the wine, the substance of these elements is changed into the substance of the body of Christ. Section 1376 of the catechism declares: "By the consecration of the bread and wine there takes place a change of the whole substance of the bread into the body of Christ our Lord and of the whole substance of the wine into the substance of his blood. This change the holy Catholic Church has fittingly and properly called transubstantiation."

What supports this remarkable declaration? What supports the idea that there are now little pieces of Christ's body in the tabernacles of Roman Churches? What is there in the Bible that gives the slightest support to the requirement that people bend their knee in worship when they come into the presence of these sacred elements?

What has happened in the development that has culminated in the theory of transubstantiation to explain how the bread and the wine are changed into the true body and blood of Christ is not hard to understand in the light of the way human beings always create religion that is appealing to them. Human religion that is not based on the Bible always manages to worship the creature, rather than the creator, as the Apostle Paul declares in Romans 1:25. When we study the phenomenology of religion we observe that all non-biblical religion creates artifacts, holy objects, and various material things that become the focus of attention for the faithful. Followers of these religions bow to these objects, light candles in front of them and, in some cases, carry them on their persons. When the mysteries of religion are concentrated in certain material objects, the ordinary worshipers are freed from trying to understand the mysteries of their religion themselves; all they need to do is focus on the objects their religion presents to them.

A striking example of this is found in the history of the people of Israel who developed an interest in worshiping a bronze snake call Nehustan; I referred to this earlier. God instructed Moses to lift the snake on a pole when the Israelites were dying of a plague God brought upon them to punish them for rebelling against him. When the people looked at the snake, they were healed—Numbers 21:4-9 records this history. The Israelites worshiped that bronze snake for many centuries until a godly king purified their worship and destroyed all the religious artifacts they had collected, including the snake. (2 Kings 24:8) No other people had received a clearer revelation that they were to worship God without using material objects of any kind, but Israel turned to idols repeatedly. The desire for holy objects is ingrained in human nature. This is the way we are wired, and the way we are wired short circuits biblical religion. The Bible alone keeps us on the right track.

I realized that the church had gone the wrong direction when it developed the idea that the bread and the wine of the mass is turned into Christ's true body. There is nothing in the Bible that supports this. To be sure, Jesus said, "This is my body," when he gave his disciples the bread of the Holy

Supper the first time it was served. But there are no biblical citations that support the idea that the bread he offered them was actually his very own body. The bread *represented* his body. The wine *represented* his blood. They did not *become* his body and blood.

Now you may think that a form of Christianity that does not have the mass at its center would be very un-interesting and un-inspiring. The mass is presented with great solemnity; it is truly an awesome moment in the liturgy when the bell is solemnly rung as the sacramental elements are believed to change into the real body and blood of the Lord. What happens to worship when this is removed? Who would ever want to be part of a church that does not consecrate the Eucharist? As it turned out, when I discovered the true meaning of the Holy Communion, the Lord's Supper, my life was wonderfully enriched.

Let there be no mistake: Holy Communion, the Eucharist, the Lord's Supper, is an extraordinarily important element in the church's life, and the church I am now a member of stresses this. But the view of the Lord's Supper is fed from the data of the Bible, not from the wellsprings of tradition.

The Gospel according to John, chapter 6, is a key chapter in our understanding of the Lord's Supper. In it Jesus declares that it is necessary for believers to eat his flesh and drink his blood.

Jesus said unto them, "I tell you the truth, unless you eat the flesh of the Son of Man and drink his blood, you have no life in you. Whoever eats my flesh and drinks my blood has eternal life, and I will raise him up at the last day. For my flesh is real food and my blood is real drink. Whoever eats my flesh and drinks my blood remains in me, and I in him." (verses 53-57)

This is startling language, and it left those who heard Jesus' words confused. Even Jesus' disciples raised serious questions about what he had said. Jesus then explained the meaning of his realistic language.

"Does this offend you? What if you see the Son of Man ascend to where he was before! The Spirit gives life; the flesh counts for nothing. The words I have spoken to you are spirit and they are life." John 6:61-63

With this, Jesus lifted these words out of the realm of the material and declared that he was speaking about spiritual realities. Biblical religion is spiritual; it does not focus on material objects. Several months after Jesus made his startling declarations in John 6, he instituted the sacrament of Holy Communion and said to his disciples, "This is my body," when he passed the bread of the sacrament to them. Later, as they reflected on what had happened, they realized that their "last supper" with him had become the fulfillment of the realities he had described to them earlier in John 6. They understood that they were involved in a spiritual event and that the elements represented Jesus' body and did not actually change into his body.

It is absolutely necessary to hold the Lord's Supper as it is described in the Bible in the highest esteem. Great blessing that comes into believers' lives when they partake of the sacrament in faith. But these sacramental benefits are not automatic—they do not operate *ex opere operato*, as Rome says, but depend on the faith life of the communicants. As the Apostle Paul says, "A man ought to examine himself before he eats of the bread and drinks of the cup. For anyone who eats and drinks without recognizing the body of the Lord eats and drinks judgment on himself." (1 Corinthians 11:28-29)

In the church I now attend, we prepare for the Lord's Supper by examining ourselves during the week before we go to the table. And you will notice in the sentence from 1 Corinthians that the Apostle Paul establishes a close relationship between the elements of the communion and the body of Christ. They are very close indeed, but the closeness of the elements and Christ's body are not expressed in terms of material reality but in terms of spiritual reality. As Jesus said in John 6: "The words I have spoken to you are spirit and they are life."

Recognizing that the startling words of Christ in John 6 that say that it is necessary to eat his body and drink his blood refer to spiritual reality rather than material reality lifts the sacrament to the highest wonder. At the time of the Protestant Reformation, those who rejected the mass did not reject the real presence of Christ in the sacramental event. What they rejected was *transubstantiation*, the theory that declared that when the priest consecrated the sacramental elements they literally changed into the substance of Christ's body and blood. Martin Luther did not reject the real presence of Christ in the sacrament, nor did John Calvin. John Calvin believed that he was most assuredly united with the glorified Christ in the sacrament, but he declined to offer any theoretical explanation for this wonder. For him, it was all a matter of faith. The Protestant Reformers who believed in the real presence did not believe that the substances were actually transformed into something they were not before.

One of the Reformation Confessions, the Belgic Confession, points out that God has sent the living bread "for the support of the spiritual and heavenly life of believers." It declares that Jesus Christ nourishes and "strengthens the spiritual life of believers when they eat Him," and then it explains that this eating occurs "when they appropriate and receive him by faith in the spirit."

This confession, which is one of the confessions of the church I am now a member of, describes Holy Communion in a way that emphasizes that when we partake of the sacrament in faith, we are truly united with the glorified body of Christ. Article 35 of that Confession says:

"In order that he might represent unto us this spiritual and heavenly bread, Christ has instituted an earthly and visible bread as a sacrament of His body, and wine as a sacrament of His blood, to testify by them unto us that, as certainly as we receive and hold this sacrament in our hands and eat and drink the same with our mouths, by which our life is afterwards nourished, we also do as certainly receive by faith (which is the hand and mouth of the soul) the true body and blood of Christ our only Savior in our souls, for the support of our spiritual life."

This article continues and explains just how serious it is about our actually communing with the very body of Christ.

"[Jesus Christ] works in us all that He represents to us by these holy signs, though the manner surpasses our understanding and cannot be comprehended by us, as the operations of the Holy Spirit are hidden and incomprehensible. *In the meantime we err not when we say that what is eaten and drunk by us is the proper and natural body and the proper blood of Christ. But the manner of our partaking of the same is not by the mouth, but by the spirit through faith.* Thus, then, though Christ always sits at the right hand of His Father in the heavens, yet does He not therefore cease to make us partakers of Himself by faith. This feast is a spiritual table, at which Christ communicates Himself with all his benefits to us, and gives there to enjoy both Himself and the merits of His sufferings and death: nourishing, strengthening, and comforting our poor comfortless souls by the eating of His flesh, quickening and refreshing them by the drinking of His blood." (Emphasis added)

When I was a Roman Catholic, I felt that attending mass and partaking of Holy Communion regularly was important—at least this is what I had been taught. Sometimes I attended mass just as a matter of routine. But there were times, I admit, when the grandeur and the overpowering solemnity of the occasion touched me. And some might think that I must be missing a great deal, now that I do not attend mass anymore. In fact the opposite is true.

In the church I now attend, we use a Reformation catechism that guides us as we study the Bible. There are several questions and answers that emphasize the high wonder of the Lord's Supper. There are a couple of questions that deal with the fact that God's people are truly nourished with Christ's body when they partake of the bread and wine of the Eucharist. One of the questions reads: "What does it mean to eat the crucified body of Christ and to drink his poured-out blood?"

This is the answer given in the *Heidelberg Catechism*, Answer 76: "It means to accept with a believing heart the entire suffering and death of Christ and by believing to receive forgiveness of sins and eternal life. But it means more. Through the Holy Spirit, who lives both in Christ and in us, we are united more and more to Christ's blessed body. And so, although he is in heaven and we are on earth, we are flesh of his flesh and bone of his bone. And we forever live on and are governed by one Spirit, as members of our body are by one soul."

This catechism emphasizes that the bread and the wine are not changed into the actual body and blood of Christ. But the Heidelberg Catechism goes on and asks why it is that Christ calls "the bread his body and the cup his blood," if it is not actually turned into the very substance of his body. The catechism's answer again emphasizes that we are united to the glorified Christ when we partake of the sacrament. This is what Answer 79 says: "Christ has good reason for these words ["this is my body, etc.]. He wants to teach us that as bread and wine nourish our temporal life, so too his crucified body and poured-out blood truly nourish our souls for eternal life." Then the catechism adds: "But more important, he wants to assure us, by this visible sign and pledge, that we, through the Holy Spirit's work, share in his true body and blood as surely as our mouths receive these holy signs in his remembrance, and that all of his suffering and obedience are as definitely ours as if we personally had suffered and paid for our sins."

Often we get the impression that the Reformation was a time when people threw all of the great teachings of the Roman Church away, rejecting everything. There were some who did that. But there are many churches that retain much of the truth that was a part of the catholic church throughout the centuries. And one of the great truths of biblical Christianity is that believers in Christ are united to Christ in what we call the *mystical union*. The Lord's Supper is a sacramental means that the Holy Spirit uses to fortify this holy union. Every time we go to the Supper, our pastor takes time to remind us of its meaning by simply reminding us of how important it is to partake of the bread and fruit of the vine. One of the formularies we use in our church as we approach the table contains this blessed paragraph: "Our Lord promises...that as we eat the bread and drink the cup, we are fed with His crucified body and shed blood. To this end He gives us His life-giving Spirit, through whom the body and the blood of our Lord become the life giving nourishment of our souls. Thus he unites us with Himself and so imparts the precious benefits of his death to all who partake in faith." "Celebration of the Lord's Supper," *Psalter Hymnal, p. 979-980)*

As we have seen, the Lord's Supper is extremely important for the life of the church. The Roman Catholic Church has rightly emphasized this. But over the centuries it developed views of this sacrament that are in grave need of correction. The idea that the substance of the sacrament is turned into the actual body of Christ has led the church in an idolatrous direction. It pains me to say this, but this conclusion is unavoidable. The church speaks explicitly of worshiping the elements. (*Catechism of the Catholic Church*, section 1418, p. 395). That worshipers are instructed to genuflect toward the tabernacle that contains what they are told are the actual body of Christ is an expression of this worship. Because of the reality of the substances (the species) the very offering of the sacrifice is viewed as beneficial for those who attend mass and also for those who have already died.

The Roman Church's teaching that the sacrament of the mass is effective regardless of the faith of the recipient and regardless of the faith and conduct of the celebrant, so long as he is an ordained priest, has made the church a dispenser of grace in a manner similar to the way a secular institution might dispense a natural product.

At the time of the Reformation, believers returned to the Scripture and made the Scripture alone the source of their understanding of the holy sacrament. They were freed from the ideas that had bound them to the mass and for the first time were allowed to experience the depth of spiritual blessing the biblical understanding of the sacrament provides. For me, it was a liberation to benefit from fullness of God's sacramental grace in place of the deadening superstition that had long obscured the wonder of this divine provision.

Good, wholesome religion is biblical religion. Religion that is the product of human creativity leads us on paths that may be interesting, even impressive, but they do not free our souls and point us to glory. The Roman Catholic mass is the product of tradition. Those who are truly seeking for God and the salvation he offers, need to turn aside from the mass and discover the biblical sacraments.

XIII

WHAT DIFFERENCE DOES IT MAKE?

I expect that some of you who have been reading this have been convinced in some degree at least that there is much about Roman Catholicism that is bad religion. That is, it's bad because it is a human fabrication rather than a teaching that is based on the Bible. It's also bad because Rome's religious system is causing many people to make wrong religious choices. Rome's teaching about human free will supports our self-esteem, its teaching about Mary is winsome and its teaching about the mass enables the church to maintain a strong grip on its members.

Why would anyone change this system? We cannot expect church leaders to change something that continues to make the Roman Catholic religion the most influential single religion in the world, with more than one billion people counting themselves part of this church—well over half of all Christians world-wide. Why change a system that promises to continue in its state of dominance throughout this century?

And if there is no reason to expect that this enormous church will change its basic teachings, why should you change if you are a Roman Catholic? True, there may be some elements of its teachings that are not exactly what they ought to be, but that is true of all forms of religion. I suppose I would have to admit that not everything about the church I am now a part of is exactly what it ought to be either. So why should you change?

These are natural questions, and usually the way people answer them keeps them right where they are. They don't change. They just stay put. But it is not just these natural questions that come up that tend to make people stay where they are, but nowadays especially, people assume that religion is not really that important. What religion you follow doesn't matter so long as you follow some kind of religion.

This is an age of relativism. We assume that people enjoy a wide variety of things and life styles, and no one is supposed to make any judgment about what anyone likes or does. So what if some people are attracted to a form of religion that is characterized by ritual, drama, images, candles and tradition? On the one hand we have highly structured forms of religion and on the other we have very austere, simple forms of religion…like the Quakers, for example, who sit quietly in a sparsely furnished room until someone feels moved to say something religious. Certain types of people like one kind of religion while other types of people like other kinds. Why sweat it?

In other words, what is really at stake here? Anything at all? You might be inclined to say: "Joe Serge obviously had a significant pilgrimage, but why should I follow him? Why go to the trouble of making a move? It's not fun to leave a form of religion that has been supporting your life as long as you can remember. And if you do leave, where would you go? Joe Serge ended up as part of a church that stands in the Reformed tradition, but who is to say that that's where I should end up? Religion is complicated, and different kinds of people are bound to go different directions." Different strokes for different folks, as we say.

On its deepest level, the question is this: are there things about Roman Catholic teaching that could cause a person to go to hell? That is really a nasty question, and for anyone to raise it seems very impolite. Nowadays most people don't think there is anything about any religion that is so wrong that some one who believes it and lives it will go to hell. The reigning orthodoxy these days is that religion has nothing to do with eternal salvation. It is an age of Universalism, which means that everyone will surely make it into heaven some way or another, if there is a heaven. It is generally believed that what religion you follow has nothing to do with whether or not you go there.

If Universalism is true, then it doesn't make any difference whether a person is a Hindu or an Appalachian snake handler. And if you think Universalism is true, why would you ever consider leaving a religion that you like and makes you feel good? But do you really think that Universalism *is* true? If you are a Roman Catholic, you know that your church has built its strength on the fact that most people are scared to death when they think about death and look beyond the grave. The Bible says that every one must die once and after that he will face the judgment. (Hebrews 9:27) There's something inside us that knows that that is the truth. The Roman Church makes very clear that not everyone is going to be saved, and that is why it teaches its members certain doctrines that are supposed to enable them to survive the judgment and make it through to glory.

The truth is that even though there seems to be a consensus that all religions are the same in terms of whether or not they will deliver you into some sort of bliss after you die, within most people there is an inescapable sense that the way we live in this world will have some bearing on what happens to us after we die.

After the tsunami that snuffed out so many lives around the rim of the Indian Ocean, several leaders of various religions were asked how they saw God in relation to this horror. One of them, a Buddhist, said something like this: well, the people who were killed had bad karma. Because this religion teaches re-incarnation, this leader explained that the tsunami victims had likely made some serious errors in previous lives and a few in this life as well, so they were taken out of this life so that they would have a chance to do better in the next one. Most non-Buddhists would have difficulty swallowing something like this, but most of us cannot escape the basic idea here: there is a relation between what we do in this life and the life (or lives) that are to come.

That this life is very important for what happens to us after we die is a major teaching of the Bible, as you very likely know. In the Old Testament this idea is already present. For example, Psalm 16 concludes on this jubilant note: "You have made known to me the path of life; you will fill me with joy in your presence, with eternal pleasures at your right hand." In the New Testament the idea of the resurrection is very strong.

Anyone who is the least bit interested in Jesus should understand that Jesus talked about our eternal future a great deal. When he did, he did not hesitate to tell people that not everyone is going to go to the same place. John 5:24 is an example of Jesus' teaching regarding our future existence. This is what he said: "I tell you the truth, whoever hears my word and believes him who sent me has eternal life and will not be condemned; he has crossed over from death to life."

Jesus presents himself to us as the person who will make the ultimate difference in determining whether our eternal future will be "eternal pleasures" as Psalm 16 describes it or eternal misery. In John 5:28-29 he continues and says: "Do not be amazed at this, for a time is coming when all who are in their graves will hear his voice and come out—those who have done good will rise to live, and those who have done evil will rise to be condemned."

Actually, when Jesus talked about the future of people like us, he made very clear that not all people will go to heaven. Matthew 13 has the record of a couple of stories he told that are very shocking. In one of them, he describes two kinds of people in the world, "the sons of the kingdom," and the "sons of the evil one." Then he says: "As the weeds are pulled up and burned in the fire, so it will be at the end of the age. The Son of Man will send out his angels, and they will weed out of his kingdom everything that causes sin and all who do evil. They will throw them into the fiery furnace, where there will be weeping and gnashing of teeth. Then the righteous will shine like the sun in the kingdom of their Father. He who has ears to hear, let him hear." (Matthew 13:40-43)

I have cited just a few places in the Bible that describe the fate of unbelievers in terrifying terms. For me, during the years I spent as a devout member of the Roman Catholic Church I viewed the church as that which was able to help me avoid the fire. I did not want to spend forever gnashing my teeth. I realized that *fire* and *teeth gnashing* were figures of speech, but I had enough sense to realize that they referred to something that actually existed. The Roman Catholic Church is entirely correct when it takes eternal condemnation very seriously. I took this seriously when I was a member, and I still do.

Well, if hell is real, just as heaven is real, and if the Roman Catholic Church provides a way of escaping hell, why would anyone leave it? Let's just say, for purposes of discussion, that the Roman Church provides a way of escape from this terrible fate, and the church I am now a part of does the same. Surely there are some mistaken notions in the Roman Church, but there are some in every church. So, again, the question is this: what difference does it really make whether a person is part of one church or another? So long as a person sincerely believes in some form of Christianity, isn't that person safe?

People talk this way and they think this way. But, good friend, the reason I have gone to the trouble to put this book in your hands is that I have come to see that the Roman way of salvation is not the biblical way of salvation, and it is, therefore, not dependable. As we have seen, time and time again, the Roman way consists of material taken from the Bible plus something that human beings have created. The

Roman way is the way of the Bible plus tradition. The huge tradition component in Roman Catholicism puts its members in grave spiritual danger.

When people are in danger, they should be aware of it and should do whatever is necessary to reach a place of safety. Now, there are certain religious teachings that do not place a person in spiritual danger. For example, some Christians believe that we may, even should, baptize infant children of believers while other Christians believe that we should baptize only those who have repented and confessed their faith in Jesus—older children and adults. This is a serious difference, and one's position on this issue has vast implications for many elements of faith and life. I believe that we should baptize the infant children of believers, but I would never say that those who believe otherwise are in spiritual danger. Whether we baptize infants or older children and adults is not a critical issue so far as salvation is concerned.

But there are teachings that are very critical when it comes to our eternal salvation, and it is of utmost importance that we get those teachings right. The reason I have gone to the trouble of describing my pilgrimage from Roman Catholicism to faith in Christ alone for my salvation is that I believe that there are many people in the Roman Church who will not be saved because they have been led astray by the false teachings of the church. Religious teaching is extremely significant because, if it is not true, it has the potential for isolating people from the finished work of Christ. And it is only Christ's blood—his finished work on the cross—that can save us.

If you are a Roman Catholic, you are aware I suppose that the Roman Church also understands that false religious teaching can cut people off from God's saving grace. In fact, there are spiritual teachings contained in what we call the early ecumenical creeds that the church I now attend believes in as strongly as the Roman Church does. Creeds like the Creed of Nicea, the Athanasian Creed and the Creed of

Chalcedon carefully express the biblical teaching of the Holy Trinity and the relationship of the divine nature and the human nature of Christ. And the church has always held that it is essential for salvation that we do not deny the truths these creeds contain. And I would agree.

The Roman Church has expressly said that if a person denies certain creeds, "let him be anathema." *Anathema*, as we have seen, means damned. "Let him be damned,"—that's what the church must say about those who deny there is one God who exists as three persons, Father, Son and Holy Spirit. The Roman Church rejects Unitarianism, a doctrine that denies that God is a Trinitarian God. And throughout the centuries, the Roman Church has kept its distance from church bodies that have a different view of Christ's natures, the divine and the human.

As a devout Roman Catholic, I always appreciated the church's emphasis on the importance of proper teaching. But I have found that the teaching of the Roman Church became seriously compromised by the doctrines it has developed on the basis of tradition. We have looked at some of them in this book. The errors the Roman Church continues to annunciate are terribly serious, and people who simply accept them and live according to them are, as I have said, in the gravest spiritual danger. Will they be saved? That is not for me to say; that will be God's judgment. But I can say that, on the basis of the Bible, many will not be. False teaching does not have a divine origin, and those who depend on false teaching for their salvation will find themselves cut off from eternal fellowship with God; they will spend eternity with the person who is the origin of this falsehood, and that will not be a comfortable place to be.

In the light of what I have just stated, we must ask if the Bible gives any example of false teaching that is so detrimental those who hold it will be damned? Yes it does. The New Testament book of Galatians has material that alerts us to the high seriousness of false teaching. The

Apostle Paul brought the gospel of salvation through Christ alone to the Galatian people, and many had believed in it. After the apostle left the Galatians, they began to modify the gospel Paul had brought to them. He had shown them that they were saved through the blood of Christ alone. The Galatians, however, added to this gospel and created another *gospel* that was not really a gospel. They said that male believers should be circumcised just as the Old Testament believers had been. Paul was aghast. Didn't they realize that if they did this they would be obligated to keep the entire law in order to be saved, and the law could never save them?

This is what the apostle wrote to them in Galatians 1:6-9: *I am astonished that you are so quickly deserting the one who called you by the grace of Christ and are turning to a different gospel—which is really no gospel at all. Evidently some people are throwing you into confusion and are trying to pervert the gospel of Christ. But even if we or an angel from heaven should preach a gospel other than the one we preached to you, let him be eternally condemned! As we have already said, so now I say again: If anybody is preaching to you a gospel other than what you accepted, let him be eternally condemned!*

The apostle is here anathematizing those who bring a gospel other than the true gospel. You see, there is only one gospel, and it is possible to so pervert it that the only reaction must be total condemnation. If you would take the time to read the powerful book of Galatians, you would discover that the reason that Paul was so adamant about the preservation of the gospel he had delivered to these people was that he knew that it had come from God. In this same chapter, he says: "I want you to know, brothers, that the gospel I preached is not something that man made up. I did not receive it from any man, nor was I taught it; rather, I received it by revelation from Jesus Christ." (Galatians 1:11-12)

I started this book by telling you how the apostle had been shipwrecked on Malta, the island from which my ancestors came. And I have also told you how he was changed from a member of the Pharisee sect that stressed salvation by keeping the law to an apostle who preached salvation by grace alone. When he wrote to the Ephesians, he summarized his entire message this way: "For it is by grace you have been saved, through faith—and this not from yourselves, it is the gift of God—not by works, so that no one can boast." (Ephesians 2:8-9) Because he knew that salvation was through the cross of Christ and that our works do not contribute one iota to our salvation, Paul was appalled when he heard that the Galatians were putting together a way of salvation that consisted of God's work plus man's work. He used the strong language of condemnation—let him be anathema—that he did because he knew that falling into a way of thinking that described salvation as the result of the cross plus our works was a fatal mistake.

When I was still a member of the Roman Catholic Church and I began to see the way of salvation laid out in the Scripture, I realized that I had to leave the Roman Church and find a church where salvation by grace alone was the ruling idea. I realized that the church I was part of had stumbled into the same trap the Christians in Galatia had fallen into. To be sure, the church was not advocating that its male members be circumcised and seek to keep the law of the Old Testament. But the church was advocating a way of salvation that contains many elements that go beyond the Bible's message that salvation is by grace alone, period. I realize that if I were to make this charge in the presence of some of the church's theologians they would argue that I misunderstand what the church teaches. I believe they would be wrong. One thing I am sure of is that to the ordinary, devout, faithful Roman Catholic believer the church teaches that salvation depends on faith plus a way of life that takes various teachings seriously that either contradict the Bible or come from a source other than the Bible.

Look at some of these teachings. The Roman Church's emphasis on free will elevates the capability of unbelievers beyond what the Bible allows. The Bible tells us that by

nature we are dead in our transgressions and sins."
(Ephesians 2:1) Because we are paralyzed when it comes to
doing any spiritual good whatsoever, our salvation depends
on God making the first move. The Bible teaches that we can
be born again only through the Holy Spirit's work in our
hearts. Salvation depends on God's action from beginning to
end. We have no merit, no goodness in ourselves
whatsoever. Salvation is by grace alone from first to last,
through and through, and any teaching that suggests
otherwise obscures our total dependence on God's electing
grace, Christ's perfect sacrifice and the Holy Spirit's life-
giving work. Teaching that detracts from these divine actions
seriously distorts God's holy revelation and puts both the
teacher and the learner in grave spiritual danger.

Another teaching that seriously distorts the Bible's
message of salvation by grace alone is the teaching regarding
Mary. As I have pointed out, I honor Mary and recognize
that her role in God's work of salvation was one of high
privilege. But the Roman Catholic teachings that have
embellished the biblical facts concerning this woman have
elevated her to a position so high that there is now talk of
identifying her as a Co-mediatrix along with her Son. Mary's
elevation is a dramatic expression of the Roman Catholic
teaching that salvation is the result of cooperation between
man and God. The achievement of salvation is not a
cooperative venture any more than successful heart surgery is
the result of the patient cooperating with the surgeon during
the procedure.

The development of the church's teaching regarding
Mary provides a clear example of the way much in the Roman
Church has been established as official dogma. Take the
claim that she was born without original sin. The church
acknowledges that Mary had to be saved through the sacrifice
of Christ on the cross just as everyone else must be saved in
this way. But it then adds that in her case, the fullness of her
salvation occurred before her birth rather than after it. Jesus'

sacrifice was applied to his mother retroactively so that she was born without original sin. Why does the church say this? There is nothing in the Bible that supports this notion. The Roman Church supports what it calls the immaculate conception of Mary on the basis of logic. It says that just as any human being would make his mother perfect before his birth if he had a chance to do so, the divine Christ made sure that his mother was perfect before he took his human nature from her. This is an intriguing idea, but it has nothing whatsoever to do with reality.

The Roman teaching regarding the Eucharist is another example of man-made teaching that has become the dominant factor in understanding the Lord's Supper. The central idea for Rome is that the Eucharistic elements are actually changed into the body and blood of Christ. The church boldly teaches the doctrine of transubstantiation as if it has been transposed directly from the pages of the Scripture when it is actually a purely human fabrication.

Transubstantiation—the teaching that the elements are changed into the actual body and blood of Christ—supplies the church with a mystical moment that has extraordinary power. To think that the true body and blood of Christ are present at the altar and that the tabernacle at the front of the sanctuary contains the actual body of Christ confers an aura of unique holiness to the service of the mass. As the catechism teaches, the church's entire sacramental system revolves around the moment when the awesome change occurs. The trouble is that all of this is the product of historic developments that have been elevated to high authority by identifying them as holy tradition. But none of this is supported by the cannon of Scripture.

A major problem with Roman Catholic Eucharistic teaching that insists that the elements of the supper are the actual body and blood of Christ is that the mass becomes a re-enactment of Christ's sacrifice. The New Testament book of Hebrews, chapters 9 and 10, insists that Christ's sacrifice of himself on the cross was entirely sufficient for the payment of the sins of every sinner who believes in him; to suggest that it must be offered up again is heresy.

The simple truth is that if the elements become the actual body and blood of Christ, what happens in the Eucharist is something that happens to Christ's body and what happens is that it is offered as a sacrifice. The Bible rejects the idea that Jesus' sacrifice can be repeated in any way. Our salvation depends entirely on what Christ did on the cross. The Eucharist is a remembrance of that sacrifice, and the bread remains bread and the wine remains wine.

What I have done in this book is show how the various elements off the Roman Church together create ideas among the faithful that contradict the biblical message of salvation. We have seen that the Apostle Paul felt obligated to oppose the false teaching that had grown in the Galatian church because the false teaching was an anti-gospel.

Could it be that the Roman Catholic Church, a church that is faithful to the Bible on many points, a church that is marvelously impressive with its papacy and numerous rites and rituals, is actually teaching a gospel that is not a gospel at all? Could this really be true?

Sadly, it not only could be true, but it is true. The teachings of this church describe a way of salvation that is opposed to the way of salvation the Bible proclaims. No one has made this clearer in recent years than theologian R.C. Sproul.

Sproul reacted to a major movement that sought to bring Protestants and Roman Catholics together. I need not comment on this movement, but I do want to share with you a major observation that Sproul made that can be helpful for us.

When we talk about salvation, we are actually talking about justification, the divine action whereby sinners are declared righteous in God's sight. How is it that God can declare a sinner to be righteous even when that person is a sinner?

Sproul pointed out that the Roman Catholic Church teaches that we are justified when we do certain things. This church provides its followers with an elaborate system of salvation consisting of following certain prescribed procedures. If a person believes the church's teachings and performs the activities that the church designates, that person will be saved.

Sproul reminds us that this approach to justification—to salvation—is not biblical. The biblical message is much different from that. It is the message that I have noted frequently in this book: Believers are saved by grace alone, through faith that is given them by God, and their salvation has nothing whatsoever to do with their own works. Their works are not the grounds for their salvation. God does not pronounce them "not guilty" because they've lived exemplary lives most of the time and dutifully confessed sins to a priest when they didn't. He pronounces them righteous because Jesus Christ took their guilt upon himself and paid for their sin, once for all, on the cross.

Jesus paid it all. We are saved through faith in Jesus. But even our faith is not one of our works: it is a gift of God.

Do you see the difference? The difference is this: the Roman Church says that the Bible plus tradition yields a teaching about salvation that involves faith plus works. The word *plus* is the important word here.

The church I am now a member of says that the Bible alone provides us with the teaching we need for our salvation and that teaching is that salvation is by faith alone. Notice the word *plus* is missing here.

I have provided this book with the prayer that many will see the great difference between Roman Catholic religion and biblical religion, and seeing that, will leave the Roman Church and find a church that exalts the biblical way of salvation.

The Church of Rome is a very dangerous place to be because its teaching regarding the way we are saved is non-biblical. I urge you dear reader, to take the Bible at its word: **believe in the Lord Jesus Christ and you will be saved.**

I have found unspeakable joy, peace and assurance as I have followed in the footsteps of the Apostle Paul, the shipwrecked messenger who told my ancestors the good news of salvation centuries ago, and you can have the same joy, peace and assurance if you trust in Christ alone.

This is the message we have heard from him and declare to you: God is light and in him there is no darkness at all. If we claim to have fellowship with him yet walk in the darkness, we lie and do not live by the truth. But if we walk in the light, as he is in the light, we have fellowship with one another and the blood of Jesus, his son, purifies us from all sin. If we claim to be without sin, we deceive ourselves and the truth is not in us. If we confess our sins, he is faithful and just and will forgive us our sins and purify us from all unrighteousness. If we claim we have not sinned, we make him out to be a liar and His word has no place in us. 1 John 1:5-10

Other *Burning Issues* Titles from Solid Ground

We are thrilled to have a new series of volumes which are written by living authors on *burning issues* facing the church and the world at the beginning of the 21ˢᵗ century. Thus far we have the following titles available:

Yearning to Breathe Free? Thoughts on Immigration, Islam & Freedom by David Dykstra is our best-selling book from 2006. It addresses the critical issues of our day from the perspective of the Bible. Pastor Dykstra has been interviewed by WORLD MAGAZINE; Dr. D. James Kennedy, and several other radio programs.

Pulpit Crimes: The Criminal Mishandling of the Word of God by James R. White sets out to examine numerous 'crimes' being committed in pulpits throughout the land every week, as he seeks to leave no stone unturned. Based firmly upon the bedrock of Holy Scripture, one "crime" after another is laid bare for all to see.

Common Faith – Common Culture: How Christianity Defeats Paganism by Joe Bianchi "presents an historical overview of culture with one intent: To demonstrate that Christianity is superior in every way to its pagan counterpart and has a powerful effect on the same. He succeeds, because Christianity succeeds. Find comfort and challenge in this compelling treatise." – Jim Elliff

Be Careful How You Listen: Getting the Most out of the Sermon by Jay Adams is a very important book that addresses a vital subject that has been overlooked by modern authors. "Wise are the church leaders who give a copy of this book to every family in their church." - Joel R. Beeke

Letters to a Mormon Elder by James R. White "…is a marvelous new study is a valuable text for Christians who talk with Mormons and is an ideal book to be read by Mormons." - Bethany House Publishers

Is the Mormon my Brother? Discerning the Differences Between Mormonism and Christianity by James R. White. "In recent years Mormon apologists and church leaders have waged an unflagging public relations campaign to try to rid themselves of the stigma of being considered a 'cult' in the evangelical community. James White demonstrates in a peaceable yet conclusive way that the divide between Mormonism and true Christianity remains an impassible gulf." – Dr. John MacArthur

From Toronto to Emmaus: The Empty Tomb and the Journey from Skepticism to Faith – A Rational and Scriptural Response to 'The Lost Tomb of Jesus' by James R. White. "James has done it again. This timely book handles the infidel ravings of people dedicated to destroy Christianity with care and precision. It is a devastating refutation of an outrageous claim." - Dr. Jay Adams

Other Titles from Solid Ground Christian Books

In addition to *Two Men From Malta* we are honored to offer several titles especially for the woman of God.

Famous Women of the Reformed Church by James I. Good is one of our very latest titles which is dedicated to the ladies whose lives have been used of the Lord in the building of his church. Here you will meet the wives of some of the great Reformers, such as John Calvin, Ulrich Zwingli & Heinrich Bullinger.

Stepping Heavenward by Elizabeth Prentiss has been a favorite of women all over the world since it first appeared 140 years ago. It is fictional journal of one woman's journey from this world to the next. Elisabeth Elliot wrote the Foreword that introduces this life-changing classic for all ages.

More Love to Thee: The Life & Letters of Elizabeth Prentiss by George Lewis Prentiss is the moving biography of gifted servant of God.
"It reveals the character of a woman who loved God and earnestly sought to help others to love Him." - Elisabeth Elliot

Golden Hours: Heart-Hymns of the Christian Life by Elizabeth Prentiss is the rarest of her works. "Elizabeth Prentiss did not squander her suffering… In this gem of a book, she gives us a glimpse not only of the treasures she mined but of her darkness, providing a backdrop against which those treasures sparkle all the more brightly. What a gift!" – Susan Hunt

Mothers of the Wise and Good by Jabez Burns was the very first title published by Solid Ground back in early 2001. This new edition is the best ever published. In the words of John Angell James, "It is a useful and valuable work, replete with instruction and encouragement..it deserves to have a wide circulation."

The Mother at Home: Raising Your Children in the Fear of the Lord by John Abbott is a classic that should be read by every mother who desires to raise children for God.

Woman Her Mission and Her Life by Adolphe Monod, who is best known for his book *Monod's Farewell* which was published most recently by Banner of Truth. Monod was considered the most gifted preacher in the Reformed Church in France. This volume is the substance of two sermons preached to the congregation in Paris in February 1848. Powerful and penetrating.

The Excellent Woman as Described in Proverbs by Anne Pratt is one of our latest titles for women. It is introduced by William B. Sprague, who said, "the more widely it is circulated, the better for the country and the world."

My Mother – A Story of Maternal Influence by John Mitchell is a precious account of the lasting influence a godly mother can have upon her family, and the world. "It is one of those rare pictures painted from life with the exquisite skill of one of the old masters, which so seldom present themselves to the amateur."

Old Paths for Little Feet by Carol Brandt is a manual to assist both mothers and grandmothers in the glorious task of training little ones for God.

Call us Toll Free at **1-866-789-7423**
Visit our web site at **www.solid-ground-books.com**